VENTURE

Venture

The Rogue Expeditions Story

SEÁN MEEHAN

Wandering Press

CONTENTS

Copyright © 2021 by Seán Meehan

All rights reserved. No part of this book may be reproduced in any manner whatsoever without written permission except in the case of brief quotations embodied in critical articles and reviews.

First Printing, 2021

Prelude

The sky was turning into a slate grey block as freezing winds blew off the glaciers and frozen mountain peaks of Alberto De Agostini National Park in Tierra del Fuego in the southernmost reaches of Chile. The last chinks of blue sky gave way to grey clouds, just as the last stretches of open water were closed in by drifting ice on one of the fjords of the archipelago. A calving glacier had shed a vast quantity of ice just a few moments earlier to wedge the fjord full of broken icebergs for hundreds of yards out from the glacier face. In the midst of this icy jigsaw puzzle, two splashes of black, inflatable zodiac boats about 100 yards apart from one another. Just far enough apart so that the words being shouted from one boat to the other were being stolen away in the wind.

"The big boat is going to come and rescue us!" Shouted Gabe Steger, one of the tour guides leading the excursion, trying to inform his clients on the other zodiac. "Stay calm and wait right there!" He cupped his hands around his mouth shouting out across the vastness of the fjord in vain.

The zodiac captain on Gabe's boat jabbered away in rapid Spanish on his radio relaying the information back to a larger vessel that both of the tourist zodiacs had become stuck fast in the ice - 'Shackletoned' if you will. Just a few minutes previously they had been close to the glacier face snapping pictures of the stunning blue ice and enjoying panoramic views of the surrounding wilderness with clear skies and cheery sunshine - not a care in the world, just a group of runners having some downtime between runs.

"Umm...I don't think they hear you Gabe," offered Allison Macsas, Gabe's fiancé who was co-leading the excursion.

They could just about make out figures on the other zodiac frantically poking and shoving chunks of ice with oars trying to make some forward progress through the ice jumble. Gabe and Allison huddled together on their zodiac and reviewed the situation for a moment. The boats were stuck fast in the ice with their group of clients split between the two. They, the responsible guides, have both ended up on one zodiac. Mistake. The Chilean captain on theirs spoke some English and so could keep everyone calm and informed. Good. The captain on the other zodiac, the one with the people trying to stab icebergs with an oar, spoke zero English. *No bueno.* There was a bottle of whiskey on this zodiac, quickly passed around to keep spirits high and chests warm. *Excellente!* The other had no whiskey and even had a couple of people wearing running shorts. Ay yi yi...

As if on comedic cue the sky darkened further, the breeze stiffened, and it began to spit rain. Everyone on the boat pulled coat zippers up to their noses, shoved gloved hands under armpits, and they grinned and grimaced at each other in acceptance of the fact they would be toughing it out here for at least an hour until the big vessel could come fetch them from the ice. "At least we aren't on the other zodiac!" Someone joked after enjoying a slug of whiskey, to general laughter all around. Gabe and Allison contributed no laughter, instead making eye contact for a few seconds with wry smiles.

So much can be communicated with the eyes in such a moment, especially between two people who have known each other for years and worked together through thick and through thin to build their own business from scratch. This eye contact said, 'What the actual fuck?!' It may even have asked 'how did we end up here?' Just two dreamers from Austin, Texas, in charge of a group of runners who had flown all the way to the end of the world in Patagonia to explore the landscape and the culture through running. That was what Rogue Expeditions, the start-up adventure tourism business founded by Allison and Gabe, offered. Says so right there on the box - unforgettable running adventures! Well this particular moment was certainly an adventure, it involved absolutely no running at that precise moment, but it certainly would be unforgettable for all involved. 'We'll laugh about this someday, right guys?' Gabe probably thought to himself as he scanned the faces on his zodiac, mostly hidden now by an assortment of hoods, hats and buffs.

Let's leave our 21st century Shackletons on ice and get to that question within the eye contact - 'how did we end up here?'

* * *

I became entwined in the Rogue Expeditions story years after that episode in the fjords of Patagonia. As the pages ahead will show the company and concept grew and ever more characters got brought into the fold. My own crossing of paths with Allison and Gabe in 2016 was largely fortuitous and random - that story comes later - and thanks to it, I have had the great privilege of becoming the third wheel of the enterprise. Over the last couple of years I've probably spent more time on the road guiding trips with either Allison or Gabe than they have spent together as a couple. As such, I have a unique perspective in our little nomadic family. Our nomadism, and indeed the world at large, stood still when that virus arrived and changed things forever in March 2020. The subsequent months have been itchy and frustrating for those of us with vagabond inclinations. During the enforced downtime I returned to an idea the three of us had joked about many times - a Rogue Expeditions book.

Typically this concept had come up in the context of sharing 'stories from the road' with groups we were guiding. Tour groups invariably want to hear the funny stories of previous groups, and the moments when it all seemed to be going wrong. We've told many of these stories so many times that they are now as polished and refined as any stand-up comic routine. We enjoy telling them and reliving them, joking that such and such a story from the early days of the company will be in 'chapter 2 of the book.' The anthropause of the pandemic left me thinking a little more deeply about the concept. Rather than just the funny stories or near-miss travel disasters, I thought about the things that seem to consistently and deeply interest the runners that come on our trips. They want to hear about how we came to work as tour guides, and what we did for work before, about how the company started, and where we see it going in the future. Being a tour guide, particularly on any adventure that lasts several days and especially as part of a small start-up company, is partly about giving yourself over to the people in your group. People want to hear your story and, by the same token, the whole group shares their stories. Those are the best bits of spending a week or ten days running together in an exotic land with a group of like-minded people. Sure, the running and the landscapes are great, but it is the stories we share that endure. So, I started to write. To tell all of our story. To share stories about the good days and the bad, the funny stories and the painful ones, to pull back the curtain of the life of running a small adventure tourism business. To share the who, what, when, where, and why of Rogue Expeditions. In the process I 'interviewed' Allison and Gabe repeatedly. I sent them emails with questions about the early days before my time. In response, they got themselves some adult beverages and got the voice recorder rolling on their phones. They were in Bend, Oregon, and I was initially in Ireland and then in Germany during 2020, and we struck upon an unusual cadence of conversation that worked. The chapters started to flow. We hope you enjoy them. Let's start at the beginning.

| 1 |

A Happening in the Desert: Morocco

"Sometimes some French people come here to the desert, they run, I drive, and I give them water."

HAMID

March 2012

The name Ouarzazate, a small city in the southeast of Morocco, means 'the place without noise' in the local Berber dialect. Think Morocco and many tourists will think of the hustle and bustle of crowded *souks* or marketplaces. They'll imagine hearing the cries of street hawkers pushing their trolleys full of wares around the narrow streets of Marrakech or Fez or Meknes. These traditional marketplace cities of Morocco are an assault on the senses.

Noises, smells, and amazing sights compete for your attention and most tourists end up a bit bewildered for their first day or two. A 'place without noise' seems a bit incongruous amongst these mental images.

Most tourists probably won't make it to a city like Ouarzazate. Guide books will give the city short shrift in their pages, perhaps mentioning just the key functions like ATMs, hospitals, restaurants or basic hotels. Those things that a traveller in need might require on their way south to the sands of the Sahara Desert; itself perhaps Morocco's top attraction. Indeed in terms of mass tourism Ouarzazate is usually merely a stop off point for coach loads of tourists streaming south from Marrakech on gleaming, air-conditioned, Pullmans. The tourists, mostly retirees from Europe or China, will file off into a restaurant for pre-ordered lunch menus and perhaps some light cultural entertainment; dancing or traditional music amongst the tables whilst they eat. Fed and watered, the tour groups will file back onto their coaches to point their cameras out through the tinted glass windows once more as the fleet advances on its final destination - Merzouga, the largest area of desert camps and hotels anywhere in the Sahara Desert. This is quite a statement to reflect upon. The Sahara is truly vast, about the same size as the contiguous United States. Yet so much of the Sahara region is politically unstable so as to make mass tourism relatively inaccessible, thereby making Morocco the oasis of peace in the desert.

The mass tourism route of coaches from Marrakech to Merzouga and back is a truly finely honed machine. At least it is now, at the time of writing in 2020, but in March 2012 it still had a way to go on that journey. Ouarzazate was definitely still 'without noise' and two off-the-beaten track type travellers were in town and plotting their next move on their Morocco trip. Allison, Texas born and bred, along with Gabe, St Louis born and Texas reared, were seasoned travellers by March 2012. They had honed their travel 'spidey-sense' through separate stints in Europe and South America, then later together during a year spent traveling throughout much of Thailand, Cambodia, Vietnam, Laos, and Malaysia. One becomes savvy and slightly contrarian the more one travels. Determined to resist the obvious path, dedicated to finding your own way, endlessly curious for hidden gems. Allison and Gabe were perhaps following the Lao Tzu school of thought at this point. 'A good traveller has no fixed plans and is not intent on arriving' observed the great Chinese thinker and traveller.

They had connected on the desire to travel on their first date, no less. Match.com's algorithm did its job in crossing their digital paths late in 2007 (back when online dating was a respectable outlet focused on actually dating people) and a freaky little moment in time occurred. Within the first hour of the date, they discovered they both had plans to travel to Thailand within the next few months. Weird juju. Allison was escaping her first full-time corporate job and a long-term running injury that was driving her stir crazy, so she calculated the next logical step on life's journey was a year teaching English in Bangkok. As the ripples of the 2008 financial fallout began to be felt Gabe jumped on that wave, took a severance package from his job with a large construction firm and, after a kayaking trip through the Grand Canyon, packed a bag and headed halfway around the world to share an apartment with Allison...and a few cockroaches. As Allison remembers it for me, "We figured that if things didn't work out between us then we'd just go our separate ways, but it turned out that we were great travel companions and that even after a full year of wandering around Asia, spending 24 hours a day together and living on a shoestring, we still liked each other!"

Allison and Gabe somewhere in Thailand, 2008

After their year in Asia they returned home to Austin and re-turned to the world of full-time work. Gabe initially worked for himself doing woodworking projects but then jumped back into construction management, in various roles, not wanting his career to consume his hobby of woodworking. In the big commercial con-struction world he got to work on forward thinking, challenging projects that focused on 'green' building practices, that he describes as being, "proud to be a part of." With that pride though, came long hours and stressful completion deadlines. Gabe's friends would call him the pragmatic one. He is the guy with the woodworking shop in his garage so he can fix his own stuff, he has his ducks in a row with investments and property upkeep and is a source of advice and help to the friends and family of his inner circle.

Allison, by now injury free, was consistently logging 100 mile weeks on the roads around Austin and fully immersed in the world of elite level marathon training. "My entire life was running," she tells me, "I was working full time at Rogue Running" (an Austin-based running group and community which coached beginners all the way through to the pros) "spending my mornings training, my days at a computer writing training plans, making long run maps and managing social media, and my evenings coaching or training more." When she wasn't working or running she was probably napping - a lot. Or snacking - also a lot. Gabe, whilst in another room, became attuned to the rustling noises leaving the couch, creeping across to the refrigerator, the slight suction pull noise of the door as it opened and unveiled the calories within. This is the life of a full-time distance runner, all the hours of the day devoted to running, sleeping and eating in a continuous rotation. Allison has the frequent, if slightly odd, experience of having women come up to her if she is out and about wearing shorts and question her about her legs. As Gabe explains it, "they're asking what she did to get her legs to look like that...the answer is 10 years of running 5000 miles a year!" He laughs to himself knowing that Allison is probably trying to break this news in a more hopeful manner to the wannabe shredded calf owner.

By 2012 their Asia adventures were slipping farther down the road in the rearview mirror and the pace of life was punishing. Like many folks leading modern hectic lifestyles their candles were getting burned at both ends. Weeks and months would go flashing past and there was never a moment to really pump the brakes. Whilst there was an occasional river trip to Big Bend national park on the Texas/Mexico border or a camping trip to New Mexico, they wanted something to look forward to. A real adventure. Something to put on the calendar with a big red X beside it. Precious commodity that vacation days are to the typical US worker, they pored over

Lonely Planet books and bounced ideas back and forward about how to squeeze the most juice out of a two week break. Initial plans for Spain became Portugal which seemed more unknown, but Portugal then became Morocco which seemed more exotic and affordable. The timing would be just after a sustained period of running for Allison as she prepared for the US Olympic Marathon Trials in Houston and smashed her personal record time. The physical and mental strain of achieving this meant this Morocco trip was much needed, if not thoroughly mapped. They would just get there and wing it.

So they found themselves in the quietness of Ouarzazate, several days into their trip, hanging out in the communal area of their hotel with no fixed plans for their immediate future. They had just parted ways with some friends who had to return home, and so they were contemplating their next move. The lobby was typical of the kind found in Moroccan *riads* (family run guesthouses) with ornate lamps adorning walls and table tops, mosaic tiling covering floors and ceiling, plush hand-woven carpets displayed as wall hangings, and comfy couches and cushions for lounging on. A local tour guide dropped off a couple at the hotel reception as they watched on. It was clear genuine thanks were being given to the tour guide for an 'unforgettable experience' camping in the desert. The tour guide smiled and demurred humbly that the tourists were most welcome and please come back anytime. Allison and Gabe exchanged a little glance. This guy had a nice energy about him.

"Uh hi, do you organise desert tours?" Enquired Gabe as the local guide had one foot through the door on his way out.

"Yes sir I do, yes. I can arrange for you a driver and make camping in Chegaga dunes and I am available tomorrow." The guide responded in good English, accented but clear, with an endearing way of getting words not quite in the right order sometimes.

"OK interesting. And is that 2 nights camping or 3 nights? Food included?"

"Yes sir all is included, food, driving, camping, and all can be 2 nights or 3 nights as you like it."

Allison and Gabe exchanged another look. Usually at this point the tour guide would take a couple of steps forward and start doing a little selling. Perhaps rustle up some mint tea out of thin air and start asking the generic stock questions; where you are from? First time in Morocco? etc etc. The usual shtick. But this guide just hovered a nice social distance away.

"I mean, we are probably never going to be back in Morocco," suggested Gabe to Allison, himself still unconvinced.

"Yeah..." she chewed on her lip, "and these are the Chegaga dunes, the ones we heard about that almost no-one goes to."

They had picked up a tip a few days previously in another part of the country that Chegaga, not Merzouga, was *the* place to see the Sahara. Avoid the masses. Go where the big Pullman coaches can't go. The local guide hovered a little longer shifting from foot to foot in his traditional leather sandals.

"But it means we need to ditch going to the coast," Gabe reasoned against himself doing calculus of their remaining days in the country. The local guide fidgeted in the voluminous pockets in the front of his *gandoura,* a flowing full-length robe made of rich looking blue cotton and trimmed with decorative gold thread. On his head he wore one of the lengthy turbans typical of local desert people, several metres of dark cloth wrapped around and around the head with excess draped stylishly over shoulders like a scarf.

"Yeah..." Allison chewed the other side of her lip, "and maybe there isn't much to actually *do* in the desert."

The local guide produced a handwritten note from the pocket of his *gandoura* with his name and telephone number.

"OK so you can think about it and if you would like to go just call me," he announced with a smile ending the equivocation. His smile was warm and genuine, and having handed over the piece of paper, he spread his arms wide, palms out, as if to say - nothing more I can do folks, this is your life.

"OK, uh, thanks…." Gabe glanced at the note he had been given, "….thanks Hamid, we will discuss our plans over dinner and be in touch." If they were to go to the desert they would need to leave early the next morning, so it was imperative that they let Hamid know their decision this evening.

"Insha'Allah, thank you so much" replied Hamid as he backed out the door beaming.

"Well that was refreshing." Gabe chuckled.

In their previous two weeks in Morocco every street vendor, tour guide, taxi driver, restaurant server, and hotel owner had one thing in common - a little bit of hustle. Not necessarily the bad rip-off kind of hustle, although occasionally that too, but mostly just good old-fashioned bootstrapping hustle of the kind required to compete in the tourism market. In Texas they might say the usual tour guide could 'talk the gate of its hinges' but this guy had answered his questions politely and went on his merry way.

Insha'Allah, meaning 'if God wills it' or 'God willing' is used across the Arabic speaking world as a punctuation mark to many conversations. Sort of a non-committal disavowal of whatever needs to come next. It is in God's hands, conversation over. Of course, literal followers of Islam take these words absolutely seriously but in Morocco, where many dub their faith 'Muslim-lite', this was far from an ironclad guarantee of anything.

Allison and Gabe headed off for dinner in Ouarzazate's central square to mull over their options. On the one hand they really did want to go to see the famous sand dunes of the Sahara, spend the night camping under the stars far from civilization, perhaps even throw in a camel ride and some live desert Berber music around the evening campfire. On the other hand, their ingrained sense of traveler independence generally precluded the hiring of tour guides of any sort. Swallowing their pride and hiring a tour guide would perhaps be an admission of one chapter closing, that of years of shoestring independent travel, and another opening - that of having a real job, steady income, less holiday days, and therefore greater need to cut to the point and hire a tour guide to get things done whilst abroad. If they had another month in Morocco perhaps they would have hitched to the desert, or rode bikes, or procured an old vehicle and headed off into the sunset, but alas no, logical decision making was at hand and Hamid would have to be called.

The decision to go was made. Gabe got up from the table and headed across the square to a local mini-market that had a pay-phone, unfurled the piece of paper with Hamid's number, and punched in the number. A few crackles and bangs on the line ensued, he thought he could hear Hamid on the other end but obviously Hamid could not hear him. Gabe hung up the phone, dug in his pocket for another few *dirhams* and tried again but got the same result. It seemed God was not willing it. He headed back across the main square of Ouarzazate. Cafes in Morocco invariably have outdoor seating areas with chairs all pointing out towards the street or square. Better so as to sit with your mint tea and your cigarette, chat to your friend beside you, but all the while face out and watch the world go by.

"No go," Gabe informed Allison, "either that phone doesn't work or I got a bad line or something...no worries, I wasn't really convinced about it."

"Me neither."

Chicken and lemon *tagines,* a classic Moroccan stew dish, slowly cooked, richly flavoured and presented in the distinctive pottery bowl with a lid like a wizard's hat, promptly arrived at their table furnished with the usual copious basket of bread and they tucked into lunch. That could easily have been the end of our story. No-one would ever get stuck in the ice in the fjords of Patagonia. But just as Gabe and Allison tore chunks of bread to wipe the bottom of their empty tagine dishes - always the best part - a familiar looking man came sweeping across the square in his flowing *gandoura* and precisely arranged turban.

"You tried to call me?" Hamid inquired.

The sudden appearance of the would-be tour guide caused bread to pause, suspended, on the way from tagine dish to open mouth. Hamid went ahead and answered the unasked question of how on earth he had known they attempted to call and how he had located them.

"I had a strange call on my phone, so I called to the operator lady to ask which number called me, she told to me that it was from a shop by square, so I go to there and ask to the man, he tells me two tourists go this way. And here I am." He finished with those out-turned palms again as a flourish and punctuation mark. Almost as if delivering a magic trick. Ta-daaa.

Gabe and Allison exchanged a quick glance over their suspended bread - this is our guy. One has to recognise ingenuity when one sees it.

* * *

The next morning Hamid arrived with a driver in a Toyota Land Cruiser. He explained he didn't yet own his own car, he was saving up for one, but that driver and guide were all included in the price agreed. They headed from Ouarzazate towards the small village of M'Hamid right on the edge of the Sahara with a steady flow of facts and history coming over Hamid's shoulder into the back seat of the

Land Cruiser. Heading to the southeast in Morocco the route follows the mighty Draa valley, home to one of the largest date palm plantations in the world. In the 1970s the Moroccan government created a huge dam upstream on the river Draa, part of a wider strategy of ensuring water security across the country. Enough water still gets downstream, albeit often many feet below the surface, to grow an ocean of date palms. As the Land Cruiser sped south the palms began to thin out, initially a wide expanse of trees a couple of miles across, the oasis dwindled away. Eventually the only river was the river of tar stretching out to a shimmering horizon across the rocky, barren desert. The rockiness of the desert is perhaps one of the first and most striking aspects of the Sahara. Far more of it is rocky and rugged than is sleek sandy dunes. The local Arabic word for a rocky desert like that is *hamada*, and the plural of this, used for an area where several rocky deserts meet is *M'Hamid*. It is interesting to think about the deserts in plural. To the outsider the Sahara is one huge contiguous area of desert on the map to be reached. A single destination. To the local inhabitants the desert has many shades and many forms. Changing geology, topography, and ancient hydrological features make it a tapestry of different deserts within one whole.

Before reaching the outpost village of M'Hamid the road crossed the last ridge of the Anti-Atlas mountains - a huge swath of rugged mountain ridges that stripe Morocco from east to west. The road passed small houses surrounded by inhospitable land, jagged red and orange rocks were scattered across a landscape entirely lacking in soil. Yet still, wizened old herders with tall staffs and large hats wandered after herds of hardy goats seeking out the few tough plant varieties that sprouted seemingly straight out of the rocky hillsides. They peered towards the car as it passed, a world apart. Crossing the last road pass the view stretched off to the dusty horizon - shades of yellow and orange landscapes blurring into the indistinct distance. The road led on like a precious trail of breadcrumbs leading back to somewhere important and eventually buildings took shape out of the dusty, shimmering air.

Driving through M'Hamid they noticed military buildings and personnel before getting into the village proper. The Morocco/Algeria border was not far off and the relationship has been a fractious one, Hamid explained. He expanded on this point, clearly on a topic close to his heart. The people in the village of M'Hamid are almost all descended from nomadic Berber families that ranged through the areas on the boundary of the Sahara pre-dating the colonially established national borders. Occasional rains can bring lush greenery to the Sahara, and before the damming of the Draa, the river flowed all the way to M'Hamid and beyond into Lake Iriki turning westward and heading in the direction of the faraway Atlantic Ocean. The nomadic people knew these seasonal patterns and moved across the landscape with herds of camel and goats, tents made of thick black camel wool, and everything else they needed to survive. They favoured the mountains to the north and west in the hot summer months, seeking out valleys at higher altitudes with cool caves for refuge and forage for animals in spite of the heat. The full name of the village is in fact *M'Hamid El Ghizlane* which more or less translates as the rocky plain of the gazelles. The gazelles now though are few. Lake Iriki is a dry lake bed cracked and parched more like the surface of the moon than a lush home for gazelles to drink. The nomadic people can no longer fully be nomads. It just isn't possible. The borders separate them from nomad brethren in Algeria and Mauritania. Ancient caravan routes that criss-crossed the Sahara carrying gold from Mali and salt from Niger converged on *M'Hamid El Ghizlane* before continuing to Marrakesh and the other royal cities of Morocco to find European buyers have been destroyed. A culture and legacy of trade as great as Asia's Silk Road, gone, dust in the wind.

Abruptly the car reached the end of the road, literally. Paved road ended and rocky dusty off-road began with a bump. Allison and Gabe reached up to grip handholds on the roof of the car and rolled up the windows to prevent the billows of dust now being kicked up from getting inside. They had been underway just a few hours but were being transported more than just in the literal vehicular sense. It was like listening to an audiobook before there were audiobooks. The landscape rolled by filled with context and understanding, rich with history and intrigue. This wasn't so much 'going to the desert' as experiencing the desert. They could see it all through Hamid's eyes.

Hamid would go quiet himself for a while, seemingly enjoying the ride just as much as they were. Sunglasses tucked into the folds of his turban he hummed and sang along to local style music on the radio as the driver maneuvered the car around soft patches of sand and over rocky humps in the road. He seemed to catch himself doing this after a while, and perhaps remembering his clients in the back seat he flicked his glass up and peered into the rearview mirror to view his guests.

"How is everybody, all good?" He addressed all two of them. He had a nice way of enunciating all the syllables of the word ev-er-y-bo-dy giving it a lyrical quality.

The track the Land Cruiser was following forked often and he and the driver would often point opposite directions and exchange in quick debates in local Berber dialect. It sounded like a language being spoken too quickly. Many sounds and words crushed into each long string of a sentence. Evidently there were many ways to reach the desert camp towards which they drove. Each driver had his own internal GPS system, or as Hamid informed them NPS - Nomad Positioning System. He smiled at this, clearly enjoying the joke even though it had surely been told many times. Stunted trees sprouted out of the rocks and soft sand became more and more abundant, piled up in mounds around which the many jeep tracks navigated. Hamid told stories of sandstorms sweeping through the area that lasted for days and blocked out the sun. Even locals could get lost in such a storm and trapped in the desert.

After an hour or so of driving even the stunted trees grew scarce and before them huge sand dunes loomed on the horizon. They seemed almost arbitrary. One section of open rolling, rocky desert ended, and then abruptly, the dunes began. Heaped up hundreds of feet high and stretching for many miles. Created entirely by nature, wind patterns driving light sand particles to land in the same patterns day after day, year after year, millennium after millennium. Hamid pointed out herds of camels ahead. They looked staged. Silhouetted and shimmering in the distance, plodding along in their unmistakable form, in search of forage not obvious to those uninitiated to the desert.

They drew close to the large dunes and the Land Cruiser began to snake and sidewind in the softer, almost powdery, sand. Finally they pulled up at camp; a collection of dark woolen tents arranged beside one large tent perhaps 100 feet by 30 feet. A concrete built outhouse stood to one side with a plastic water tank perched on one side of the roof and solar panels on the other side. Rough woven carpets connected the tents with walkways protecting bare feet from the hot sands. Around the perimeter of the camp were sand berms 30 feet high giving the whole campsite an enclosed and safe feeling - it hunkered into the dunes. Hamid sprung out of the front seat of the car and opened the rear doors in a flash.

"*Marhaba!* Welcome, welcome. You are so welcome here to our desert camp!" He beamed with a wide smile, clearly genuinely happy to be at the camp. This genuine enjoyment on his part would leave an impact on Allison and Gabe. Clearly he had done this whole routine many times, but he was getting a kick out of it. He was truly enjoying having guests in his corner of the world and showing them his knowledge and his hospitality. Tour guides often can be viewed in a negative sense due to the repetitive nature of what they do, the same questions, the same stories, the same thing different day. But here was a guy enjoying the same thing every different day. It flipped the whole thing on its head.

The Sahara camp

Few places in the world can put on a show of hospitality better than Morocco. Out here in the middle of the desert Allison and Gabe would have their first experience of what can be offered from a camp stove and a carpet. As soon as they arrived there was sweet mint tea, fresh fruit and tasty nuts, biscuits, and sweet breads all arrayed on plates and delivered to them with flourish and breakneck speed. They lounged on comfy cushions as afternoon snack time merged into early dinner. A platter heaped with barbecued goat arrived, accompanied with plates piled high with potatoes, rice, green beans, carrots, beetroot, and of course bottomless bread. They ate until they couldn't eat anymore. Then more food would arrive and politeness would coerce them into another helping. After the meal they dragged themselves and their cushions outside of the communal tent into the cooling evening air. Sunset hung heavy across the dust-laden sky. Yellows became oranges and reds and then purples as the minutes passed, throbbing colours impossible to capture faithfully with a camera. Firewood arrived out of thin air and quickly there were sparks crackling off into the dusky sky. Musical instruments appeared as if out of *gandoura* sleeves and the first drum beats rolled around the camp, tentative at first, finding the groove. Bit by bit all the workers at the camp, Hamid and their driver were all beating out rhythms on percussion instruments of various kinds. It was hard to tell who was leading the symphony, or where each song began and ended, each drummer looked at the others for small cues unobvious to the outsider. The sky grew darker above and unveiled stars such as they had never seen before. Almost like gazing up at some sort of computer generated model of the universe rather than the actual sky itself. Tea and snacks continued to arrive without invitation, though now the tea was 'nighttime tea' made with chamomile - clearly the evening was drawing to a close. The drumbeats rallied to one last crescendo before finally falling silent for the evening to be greeted with enthusiastic applause.

This was an evening to be bottled, stored carefully, and savoured at length into the future. One must attempt to write the sensory details of such an experience in the hard drive of one's memories in a way that allows as full a recall as possible. A picture alone won't do it, or a video, or a journal entry. Full sensory download is required.

Somewhere in the course of the evening conversation turned to Allison and Gabe, what they did for a living, which part of America they come from, and so on. Allison spoke of her commitment to running and how she hadn't run since coming to Morocco more than a week before (a long stretch of days to go without running for a professional marathoner) due to concern about infringing on any modesty rules and, on some level, safety concerns. Hamid empathised that running through cities and towns might not be the easiest - so much traffic and exhaust fumes, cars and people not being accustomed to runners. But out here though, in the heart of the desert, there is no-one around to care!

"Sometimes some French people come here to the desert, they run, I drive, and I give them water." Hamid informed them.

"Oh nice, good idea." Allison replied.

Hamid tests out this running idea during a drive across Lake Iriki

Somewhere in the midst of the afterglow of the good food, the excellent music, the heaven of stars above, and this novel idea from Hamid, a lightbulb moment occurred. What if this wasn't the last time they visited Morocco? What if Allison advertised a running trip to the pool of athletes back at Rogue Running in Austin (a running group hundreds strong and growing)? Would people want to fly halfway around the world to run around in the desert? They would run, Hamid would drive and give water. Simple. The food and hospitality would be no problem evidently. They could run all day and eat all night if they wanted to. Allison and Gabe could do the legwork to get everything organised, the runners would just have to book their own flights and turn up on time. That would be fun, wouldn't it?

| 2 |

Ready, Fire, Aim: Morocco

"We hadn't really thought through what might happen in that scenario."

ALLISON

Back in Austin, far from the star filled skies of the Sahara, the idea that had lodged in the minds of Allison and Gabe was not shifting. Sometimes any of us can get 'the most amazing idea' whilst on holiday, possibly a bottle of wine deep at the time, and once back in normal surroundings it doesn't seem so great anymore. Many of us are guilty of scrawling a note-to-self on a piece of paper or a text note on your phone, the big idea, the game changer, but then the next day, on return to sobriety and reality, the idea is promptly consigned to the trash. On leaving Morocco, Allison and Gabe told Hamid they would be back next year with a big group of runners to go running through Morocco, camp in the Sahara, visit Hamid's family, ride camels, drink mint tea, stuff faces with tagines, the whole Moroccan nine yards.

"Inshallah we will see you again!" replied Hamid, seeming enthusiastic that they had a nice trip, but perhaps dubious of their conviction to return. This wasn't his first rodeo.

"No no seriously we *will* be coming back...we will email you, ok? So you can book hotels and drivers and everything."

"Whatever you need, you are welcome back here anytime," his response again seemed chosen from the basket of generic stock responses to overzealous tourists.

"We WILL be back. We promise. Believe us. Alright?"

"Inshallah, thank you so much."

God always has the final word anyway.

* * *

With a Moroccan tan still glowing on her cheeks Allison slipped back into life at Rogue Running in downtown Austin, Texas. Rogue Running served then, as now, as the centre of all things running in Austin. It operated then out of a downtown building - half run retail shop and half training room - that was well located so as to quickly join the trails and paths around Town Lake enabling runners to get their miles in along the Colorado River. Post-run Austinites would perhaps finish up with a dip in Barton Springs for a cool down and maybe even round things off with some breakfast tacos at Tacodeli or Torchy's. Running groups rocked up to Rogue at the crack of dawn seven days a week to trot out their miles in various pace groups. Elite athletes checking in multiple times per week for coaching sessions and strength drills and flexibility workouts.

The training room, at that time a rather cramped space for the number of athletes that gathered inside each day, featured whiteboards continually updated with weekly training plans and calendar countdowns to key races nationwide. Runners' moons orbit according to certain key marathons like New York or Berlin which might require qualification times achieved at a previous marathon. Some marathons are favoured for having fast courses or good weather conditions to run your personal best time and secure a spot at qualification only marathons like Boston. There is a cadence to the running year that dedicated runners understand. They map out their running goals weeks, months and even years in advance using Rogue as their study library.

Running related paraphernalia was often strewn across the training room floor, everything from foam rollers to trigger point sticks, resistance bands to core stability balls, and all manner of massage implements like modern version of a medieval torture dungeon. Tight iliotibial bands and shin splints were a rite of passage, intermittent knee pain and janky ankles an accepted reality. What can only be described as a 'runner smell' emanated from the closet that housed the lost and found section - socks, shoes, buffs, hats, t-shirts, towels, knee bandages, handheld water bottles, all abandoned at some moment of exhaustion and never reclaimed. Garmin GPS watches hung limp from power sockets, suspended by their charging cables, near trash cans filled with wrappers of all kinds of sugary curiosities aimed at avoiding the dreaded runner's bonk. Posters advertised upcoming guest speakers, often coaches or professional athletes, from the world of running who would regularly attend to present running workshops and question and answer sessions - almost every runner was searching for that next bit of information or insight that would make them faster, stronger, better. Near the door printouts were available with maps and explanations of upcoming training run routes. Some favourites included dreaded hill sessions - slogging up and down specially chosen steep Austin roads to build strength - or 'Long Run Saturday' which would see hundreds of runners from all over Austin pass through the doors to sync in with their group and their coach before hitting the pavement for the miles that would push their limit according to their tailored training plan. Rogue Running was a place of verve and action, sweat and effort, passion and community, all centred around the simple act of putting one foot in front of the other and getting some miles in.

Allison was part of a small team of highly dedicated and hardworking people keeping the thrum and whirr going. As well as running as a professional athlete by now for Rogue Athletic Club, the sponsored elite team of Rogue Running, she was coaching marathon groups and managing all manner of marketing tasks for the wider Rogue Running community which numbered into the thousands - email newsletters, social media updates, graphic design projects for shirts, posters, flyers, logos, you name it. At a weekly marketing meeting she pitched the Morocco idea to her boss, Ruth. Without a whole lot of thought or deliberation she was encouraged to 'put in a newsletter and see what happens.' This was typical of the can-do attitude of a bootstrapping startup like Rogue Running at the time, as well as indicative of the level of trust placed in Allison, by then several years in and a trusted cog in the Rogue machine. As Gabe puts it for me, "a running trip to Morocco sounded like a Rogue thing to do." This was the same crew that on Thursday night would lure people down to the shop with a free keg of beer, invite everyone to put on some fancy dress, and then hit the roads running around downtown Austin, drawing attention and bringing more folks into the fold to grow the business. All ideas were possible.

Hundreds of runners - a typical sight - gathered at the original Rogue Running location in Austin, Texas
AzulOx Photography

One newsletter email later, bearing a hastily assembled new logo of a runner carrying a suitcase, and the not-so-catchily named 'Running Trip to Morocco' had 22 registrants within a couple of days. So much interest that they had to cap the numbers before the group got any larger. As Allison remembers it the most exciting part was that initial ideation, the creating and the marketing of the concept, and then the excitement of getting 22 sign-ups almost straight away. That took full focus. Not until later did detailed thoughts of 'how are we going to do this' emerge. It was classic start-up style; ready, fire, aim.

Gabe at this point was lost again in the world of large commercial construction. Working against the endless procession of concrete pour deadlines, revised budgets, construction timeline overruns, and wrangling sub-contractors. Long hours were standard, stress was unavoidable, things could never be built fast enough. Anyone who knows construction sites can imagine that his co-workers probably did not appreciate his wistful travel stories about the sands of the Sahara and the culture of Morocco - there was more pressing business at hand. Allison was therefore doing most of the initial legwork on the trip - excuse the pun. Gabe's skills though would be necessary to bring the trip to life and fruition, from idea to reality. He had made some extra bucks back in his college days at Texas A&M guiding rock climbing trips and had also organised several multi-day river rafting and kayaking trips amongst friends. His love of trip planning and his inherent practicalities would offer useful balance as the concept took shape.

In his words at this stage, "there was no thought of it being a business, it was just a cool thing to do with a big group of people, that Allison and I were, y'know, *quasi* in charge of."

Some email exchanges with 'their guy in Morocco' Hamid got them a rough handle of the costs involved. They would keep it real simple. Every participant would book their own flights to Morocco, and the price of the trip would be just enough to cover the hard costs of hotels, transport and food, plus the cost of Allison and Gabe's travel. Throw a customised trip t-shirt in the bargain and they had lift-off. Allison hosted an information night for the trip at the Rogue shop so all the participants would get a chance to meet each other and they could ask questions about the details and specifics of the trip. How far will we run each day? Can I run at my own pace? What will the weather be like? Can I wear shorts when running there? The same questions which today form the foundation of the FAQs section on the Rogue Expeditions website. In truth Allison will now freely admit that she stood up there and fielded questions for which she did not have an answer. Whilst she was the only one in the room who had been to Morocco, it had not been a scouting or logistics planning trip. She hadn't even run whilst she was there! And she and Gabe had spent only three days out of their two weeks in Morocco with their 'guy in Morocco.' A lot was to hang on Hamid. Hotel choices, roads they could run on, a team of drivers, a cook team to prepare lunches, any additional activities or visits. Better hope they had picked the right guy.

Hamid if you recall correctly from the previous chapter was at this point still climbing the tourism ladder in Morocco. You hadn't made it as a driver and guide in Morocco until you owned your own Toyota Land Cruiser. He hadn't reached that level yet. Back in 2013 it wasn't so long since he was working for his uncle doing camel trekking tours to their family-owned camp in the Chegaga dunes. Contrary to every image you have in your mind of riding camels, camels actually do not like to host humans on their backs, and the desert tribes usually did not ride them. Hamid and his uncle operated their trips in traditional fashion. You loaded camping gear and supplies on to the camel and then you walked ahead of your camel, leading it by a rope. Typically they hiked across the rocky desert plateaus during the cool hours of early morning before finding some shade or refuge to languish during the hottest hours of the day. Then made some more progress in the cool of the evening before setting up camp for the night.

Hamid and his uncle had a network of multi-day routes in their minds criss-crossing their local desert to areas of beauty and historical interest. They themselves were direct descendants of the local desert Berber tribes who had crossed these desert sands for centuries. Traditionally, during the summer months especially, these Berber tribes of this area of the Sahara would have travelled by night, navigating by the stars which they knew intimately. Naturally night trekking is a harder sell for the visiting tourists. Hamid and his uncle had the stories and interpretation of the land to unlock its secrets for the intrepid visitor in search of an authentic experience. What Hamid realised though, back then in his youth working for his uncle, was that they were at the end of a very long road from the tourist cities of Marrakech or Agadir or Casablanca. The tourists seemed to all be going on coaches to Merzouga, very few arrived in their village of M'Hamid in search of camel trekking. He decided he would have to go to the tourists and intercept them.

This gives us 'the why' of Hamid being a few hours drive from home, based in Ouarzazate, scoping around for the next Allison and Gabe of this world. His strategy had worked and now he had a contact who wanted to bring more clients. Equipped with access to a new email account he was about to become the lynchpin of a dream vacation for 22 runners in faraway Austin, Texas. In the intervening months emails went back and forth about dates, hotel reservations, drive time durations, diet restrictions, roads quiet enough for nice running and wire transfers to cover the costs. On this last point of wire transfers he was taking a leap of faith with these Americans. He couldn't receive money ahead of time as he didn't have a bank account at that point. So he was relying on a rather stuffed brown envelope coming with the runners from Texas. He was calling in favours for a lot of reservations and had a lot of bills to pay!

The very first marketing photo, inspired by a bottle of wine and a crazy idea out in the Sahara

March 2013

"Where are we going next?"

This became the recurring question as the days of the first ever 'Running Trip to Morocco' began to slip away. They were already thinking about the next running trip before this first one had even ended. The 22 runners were well and truly in the flow of the daily routine of their dream running vacation. They would eat breakfast early - freshly squeezed orange juice, bottomless sweet mint tea, somewhat drinkable instant coffee, baskets and baskets of freshly baked bread, hard boiled eggs, sweet jams, and spreadable cheese packets. Their luggage would be whisked off and loaded onto the roofs of their convoy of Land Cruisers. They'd top up their water bottles and hydration bladders, pocket some fruit for their run, ensure their running backpacks had sufficient gels, bars and salt pills and then they'd hit the road. The team of Moroccan drivers, coordinated by logistics chief Hamid, would shepherd the runners along a stretch of quiet and scenic road or jeep track like collies flanking a flock of sheep. They leapfrogged along between the runners offering snacks, water, directions, and the ever-present words of encouragement to keep going, "*YALLA, YALLA!!*" Let's go, let's go.

The very first run of the very first trip!

They ran on picturesque roads against the backdrop of the snow-capped Atlas Mountains. They ran on mile after mile of open expansive high desert terrain stretching out starkly and beautifully to the horizon. They ran through deep river canyons etched into the landscape by seasonal rivers flowing south from the High Atlas. Day by day their itinerary took them further into rural southeast Morocco into ever more classical desert landscapes with rougher roads, smaller and smaller villages, sculptural rock formations, massive blue skies, and stunning sunrises and sunsets. Past date palm plantations and wheat fields, along goat trails and jeep tracks, through shimmering heat and cool crisp evenings, with sounds of warbling minarets calling the faithful to prayer and bleating sheep herds calling warning at their passing, they ran miles that let them absorb the sensory fabric of life in this part of Morocco. Some runners just wanted a couple of miles at a sedate pace before they'd flag a driver and hop in the cars to ride to the finish line whilst others were intent on cranking out ten or fifteen or more miles per day. Post-run there was always a huge lunch to replace those burned calories, ice cold swimming pools for soaking legs in recovery, maybe a little afternoon nap, or gentle walks to see some cultural sights. Dinner each evening was accompanied with an exchange of runner stories. Topics ranging through all those favourite runner topics such as losing toenails (often pluralised), battery life of GPS watches, worst chafing episodes (if your nipples haven't bled profusely you simply haven't run far enough), and more shoe talk than a Jimmy Choo product launch. Wine and laughter accompanied these dinners every evening before all retired to early slumber each night. Rinse and repeat the next day. What more could a runner want?

One runner, Devon, got so into the flow that he wanted a full marathon every single day he was in Morocco - 26.21875 miles. He would start earlier than the rest and finish later. Early in the morning and in the heat of the day he was to be found cramming in extra miles with 'out and back' additions from their hotel for the night or from their picnic lunch spots. Such a volume of running would result in an appetite of course and he learned the hard way that Moroccan dinner hospitality is a serious business. Requesting an extra piece of chicken one night at the end of an already huge group dinner he received instead a whole bowl of chicken; an entire tagine of it. No-one goes hungry at a Moroccan dinner table. Whilst the rest of the group recoiled away from the dinner table onto sofas, themselves in various states of distress with bloated bellies and tired legs, Devon tucked in like a trooper, not wanting to be impolite, and polished off the better part of the tagine. Better so as to fuel tomorrow's marathon after all.

Devon poses with the Moroccan crew at the finish line of his 7th marathon

The runners were clearly having a blast. Allison and Gabe were nominally in charge and they would give a briefing every evening about what would happen the next day - where the group would run, what town they would stay in, what sights they would see, etc. These briefings were heavily propped up by Hamid of course who supplied the specifics and local intel wherever it was required. Gabe recollects being more of a trip ambassador than a tour guide or organiser per se. He and Allison were the chief cheerleaders, but the trip was taking on a life on its own. Runners want to run, of course. They feel all warm and glowy after they run. This is the so-called 'runners high,' a real thing, a release of endorphins post-running that links our modern bodies back to prehistoric times of gathering and hunting to survive when several miles of run-walking was a daily necessity. The more you run, the more it becomes a need, a key building block of your day and your life. You think clearer, feel better, eat better, sleep better, after running. So if you do it every day, in an engaging and enchanting part of the world, where all the logistics are taken care of and you just need to wake up and run every day - this is running nirvana, right?

The group running glow even infected the Moroccan drivers. On one of the last runs Mohamed, chain-smoking, totally non-runner, non-sport of any kind, 60 something year old, joined the American runners. He trotted out several miles through the shimmering Sahara-heat dressed in long pants, dress shirt and padded waistcoat, and beat-up second-hand gym shoes. At the finish of that run, at an arbitrary gas station that, crucially, sold ice-cold Fanta and Coca-Cola, the other drivers unwound a turban and held it across the road as the finish line. Mohamed crossed the turban line to much cheering and acclaim to earn his well-earned Fanta and a cigarette. Allison and Gabe wouldn't find out until a year later that he was barely able to walk for a week after his heroic couch-to-10k antics!

Not that the trip was all running of course. For purely practical reasons running is only going to take up a couple of hours of each day. So unlike a hiking or cycling holiday which the activity can be sustained as an all day affair, there were hours left in the day for cultural activities and regular tourist stuff. The culture pit-stops took on various forms and was somewhat responsive to opportunism based on what was along the route, the ambient mood and energy level of the group, and time available that day. The group visited ancient *kasbahs* (old, fortified castles constructed from adobe) such as Ait Ben Haddou now famous for featuring in several movie productions such as Gladiator and Babel. They visited *souks* (the busy Moroccan marketplaces selling every imaginable product) to look at spices, handmade leather products and carpet weavers. They got explanations about the subsistence life of local farmers who tended goats, planted wheat and alfalfa, and sold cash crops like olives or dates. They even visited a pottery cooperative on the edge of the Sahara in the town of Tamegroute, famed for its excellent quality clay and distinctive green glazing which is concocted from a mixture containing cobalt, manganese and other rock minerals mined from the nearby Anti-Atlas Mountains. The particular green colour is particularly favoured in Morocco as it emulates the official green colour of Islam.

From the runs to the food, the cultural pit stops to the fun interaction with the driver team, and as marked by the repeated refrain "where are we going next" the trip was meeting expectations and then some. It was so novel and unique. The runners all felt they were part of something, willing guinea pigs to a brave new world of running adventure. They were all patient zero to this running and culture travel experiment. Not that everything went to plan on the travel front of course; when does it ever in the world of international travel? Someone, still unidentified, brought a little gift into the close-knit group of runners. Something the local Moroccan drivers referred to laughingly as Ouagadougou (wa-ga-doo-goo). A catchall word for any number of travel-related illnesses that can occur, from colds to bugs. Now, of course, Ouagadougou is the capital of Burkina Faso, so I hope any citizens will forgive me for what I am about to write, but the word somehow sounds like exactly the type of bug or ailment you don't want to catch. As in, "oooh, she got a pretty nasty case of the Ouagadougou." Clearly one does not want to be the "she" in our illustration. But, runners doing what runners do, sharing water bottles across multiple cars, eating with sweaty hands out of shared lunch platters, and generally keeping close proximity with one another, a little bit of the old Ouagadougou spread through the group. It manifested in different forms, all short-term, quite debilitating, and involved a bout of discharge from one or another orifice. Travel is an adventure, right? Moving swiftly along.

Another slight speed bump occurred before the trip had properly begun. All of the group had booked the same set of flights routing them from Austin to Dallas, Dallas to Madrid, and finally Madrid to Marrakech. By the time the whole crew got to Madrid some of the group figured they had earned a stiff drink. One of the group, Yvette, lost track of time, or perhaps wine, and missed the flight. And then there were 21. Everyone else arrived in Morocco and you can picture the airport head count for yourself. A text came through from Yvette saying she would get a flight the next day, but the group was already scheduled to roll out and run the next day. They wouldn't be in Marrakech when she got there.

"We hadn't really thought through what might happen in that scenario" remembers Allison. In the years to come, through dozens of trips, this would become the cornerstone of all trip planning. Thinking through the 'what ifs' of all scenarios at all times and creating plan B, plan C, all the way through the alphabet sometimes. Solving problems before they even exist is the hallmark of a good travel planner. But this is now, and that was then. Enter Hamid, of course, troubleshooter of all Moroccan problems then and every day since. Yvette arrived the next day and there was a man with her name on a sign (well almost, the spelling was wrong, but you know, close enough) outside the airport. She jumped in his car and they set off for a four hour drive through the twisty mountain road that crossed over the High Atlas mountain range to reach the southern part of Morocco. As they plunged onwards through the gathering darkness on increasing small and dusty roads, Yvette, well-travelled and streetwise it should be said, must have pondered a little on that mistaken spelling on the sign, on her aloneness and lack of phone signal, on the fact she was a single woman in car with a guy who doesn't speaking any English. But her trust was well placed, and as she recalls it, "what choice did I have once I was in the car, I figured I might as well roll with it." She caught up to the rest of the group just in time for dinner at the end of their first day, and then they were 22 again.

The highlight of the trips was to be at the Sahara desert camp of course. The group lived out Hamid's explanation of 'they run, and I give them water' running through his home desert towards the epic dunes of Chegaga. The runners spread out into a line trotting along over packed sand with a crusty top that occasionally crunched through and sapped a little momentum. They climbed over small rocky rises in the landscape only to see the next rises shimmering tantalisingly on the horizon. Running in such a place is a very here and now moment. You can't help but be absorbed by the different-ness of the place. Your entire being and consciousness is absorbed in the sound of the sand and stones crunching under your feet. You become absorbed in the sweat droplet that trickles around your eyebrow, sneaking into your eye with a sting. When a lonely blast of wind arrives to cool the sweat on your skin you grin with the momentary respite. This is like enforced conscious running for those who haven't practised it before. Just keep moving forward, keep noticing the sights and sounds, keep feeling the place you're moving through.

This mood deepened as the runners gathered after the run finish to enjoy sunset at the top of a tall dune behind the camp. They plopped onto the warm sand and gazed over a sea of sand dunes melting off to the west into an orange sky. Wine, wisely purchased with foresight in Marrakech, was liberally distributed by their campsite hosts, and swigged in between handfuls of locally produced almonds and dates. Contented sighs exuded from tired bodies after their run. Bare feet rejoiced in the silky smooth sand set free from their sweaty and smelly Hoka or Brooks prisons. Right around actual sunset the bubbling conversation (probably centred on giving updates on problematic toenails or some new muscle ache) naturally fell to a lull and all was well with the world. It can't not be in such a moment. This is when the word awesome should actually be used. The word is almost vacuous now due to its heavy overuse. But it can rightly be applied to such a moment when truly in awe of a brilliant feature of nature.

The buzz glow of the Sahara consumed the group as it had consumed Allison and Gabe the year before setting all these events in motion. As with Allison and Gabe's first visit the evening became even more atmospheric after sunset when delicious dinner was consumed, the firepit stoked high, and the drumbeats of the camel skin drums began their tattoo. The buzz did end that night in laughter and embarrassment however. After a few songs the locals, belting out song after song of traditional Berber desert music in choirly unison, ceded the floor to the visitors. What songs did they know? What music had they brought from their country to be heard here in the desert? What followed was a debacle of forgotten lyrics, false starts, and wrong keys. The American's lurched from a couple of lines of Country Roads into a garbled rewrite of Ring of Fire. No-one knew enough lyrics to lead and amongst 22 of them no consensus emerged on a song to stick with. Yousef, one of the Moroccan camp team, felt pity and began to beat out a drumbeat and sing some lyrics first to Beyonce and then Kanye West. The Americans winced in unison. Perhaps it was better if they didn't donate any musical culture to the Sahara. Finally, at the last moment, a consensus emerged and the inaugural Rogue Expeditions trip was commemorated eternally with the voices of 22 out of key runners emptying their lungs into the Sahara night sky with the timeless lyrics of Happy Birthday to You.

It was no-one's birthday, but it was the best they could do.

Bemused and amused locals listening to a group of American runners attempt a campfire song

* * *

"Looking back, I feel like I was sort of winging it on that first trip," Allison tells me, reminiscing on that beta edition. Yet they received stellar feedback from the runners on the inaugural trip. There had been 'a happening' out there in the desert. This was a strong feeling this should not be just a one-off thing. Perhaps the moment of real validation arrived with the words of praise from one of the runners, Amanda. Just before Morocco she had been to Kenya with a small company offering bespoke safari tours with a focus on community integration and sustainable tourism. She had been blown away by that trip. Now she had been blown away all over again. Even though Allison and Gabe claimed they were only *quasi* in charge it had turned out to be a hell of a trip. Hamid and his Moroccan crew had knocked it out of the park and they were delighted too. Hamid recognised at that moment that this could be the beginning of a niche for him. He had worked incredibly hard to over-deliver for these visiting American runners - he hoped more would follow, and he was right. Allison, Gabe and Hamid had struck an accord and understanding during the 10 day trip that would set them in good shape for years to come. They just got each other. Of course they would want to bring more groups back here and do it again. Were mistakes made? Of course. How else do you learn? Was there room for improvement? Absolutely. That's the whole fun of trip planning. The tweaking and changing, the sculpting and massaging of an itinerary. Those words from Amanda may have been exactly the words of validation they needed to go away feeling accomplished, feeling like they wanted to do this again.

In the afterglow of the trip Allison and Gabe started to become more sure they had stumbled across a pretty cool and novel idea. The world was going through a great opening up in terms of tourism, and especially adventure based experiential travel. People began to consider travel as a rite of passage, a part of who they would become as people. They didn't so much travel to destinations, they went on journeys to be changed, to experience and interpret, to grow and evolve. A generation was emerging that wanted experiences and not things. Previously 'making it' was evaluated based on your ability to be successful in your career, drive a good car, and own a big house in a nice area. Maybe eventually send your kids to good schools and colleges. Now the narrative was more about how well rounded an individual you were. What challenges and experiences you had overcome. Were you happy and fulfilled, motivated with your life trajectory? People began to speak of life in chapters to savour rather than as a ladder to be climbed. Each person was writing their own story and travel played a huge role in the writing, often providing key building blocks and plot lines.

Alongside these developments, and doubtless intertwined with them, Facebook moved beyond keeping in touch with old friends, the early years, to demonstrating your lifestyle choices, the maturation years. Other apps would rise. Written blogs of travellers would be replaced by vlogging on YouTube. Snapchat and Instagram offered continuous insight into how people were living their lives and immediate feedback and gratification from both known friend groups and beyond. Planning social media posts became a theme in the mind of the average traveller. A moment to share your progress. Much better than the new car or new house milestones of previous generations, these moments were regular and ongoing.

Another simultaneous development during the intervening years was the emerging plethora of choice for the would-be traveller. Flights were never so plentiful, never so cheap, and never so easy to find and book. The profession of the travel agent was obliterated by websites like Skyscanner, Kayak, and Google Flights. More and more things became digitised and bookable on the internet. Hotel rooms, rental cars, even entire homes became available on Airbnb. Against this world of information, not to travel seemed almost not a choice. Everyone was doing it. Yet at the same time, such an overload of information provided both freedom for the independent traveller and also opportunity for the innovative tour operators who could navigate all the information, separate the wheat from the chaff, and curate and organise trips that maximised experiences.

Adventure travel was of course already well established. Trekking, mountaineering, kayaking, cycling, fishing, deep-sea diving, bungee jumping, zip-lining - there was a plethora of choice. Destinations became synonymous with the activity they typically offered. You had to dive the Blue Hole in Belize, or trek the Inca

Trail, or climb Kilimanjaro. If you wanted to 'do' the campervan life, you really had to go to the South Island of New Zealand. If you wanted to 'check the box' and get your open-water dive certification, then Thailand was the place for you to do it on a dime. Throw in some tubing on the rivers of Cambodia and Laos whilst you were in the area.

In tourism things were moving faster than ever before with ever more niches emerging all the time. As quickly as Lonely Planet could publish an article on 'the next great place you have to visit' that place was doomed and a new place would emerge. As quickly as some sight or attraction became 'insta-famous' the search for the next undiscovered gem began. A segment of travellers began to seek out authentic, genuine experiences. They sought to avoid 'check the box' destinations, and 'bucket lists' and instead seek out small companies, with ethical principles, who could curate and create unique and novel ways to travel the world. Running could be one such way. As the idea crystallised in the weeks and months after the first Morocco trip, they were finally able to put it into words. Sometime after that first trip on the newly minted website of Rogue Expeditions, a sister company to Rogue Running, the blurb captured their idea as follows:

Rogue Expeditions is a unique adventure travel company that creates run-centric vacations around the world. Our itineraries are designed to combine authentic, off-the-beaten-track travel experiences with organized, supported daily runs in unforgettable places, and to accommodate all levels. Put more simply, we are adventure travel for runners!

| 3 |

A Sense of Direction: Tahoe

"Maybe you could do a trail running trip?"

NICOLE

Ask any business owner, be it a small start-up or large multinational corporation, and they will tell you about the importance of network. They may call it 'the little black book' or 'knowing the right people' or some other such euphemism. Finding the right people to work with, be it by dumb luck or careful search, defines the success, or failure, of many enterprises. The beauty of retrospect is to look back at a rich cast of characters accumulated along the way which made it all possible. To see the intricate web that builds out, conversation by conversation, introduction by introduction, from speculation to giving it a go, from first contact to teamwork and solidified trust.

Around the time of that first trip back in March 2013 two dominoes fell that would lead to the beginning of the network forming around Allison and Gabe. This new network already included Hamid and his team in Morocco, and of course the 22 runners who had guinea pigged their way through the first trip. The first domino came along with Amanda's words of praise comparing her Morocco running experience to her Kenya safari experience. To her the trips were similar in their attention to detail, friendly laid back vibes, sense of confidence that 'everything would be taken care of', and general good vibes from the trip leaders. She offered an introduction to Kinuthia who had organised her Kenya trip. Amanda had a hunch that Allison and Gabe would like Kinuthia's style. Kinuthia, born in Kenya, living in Austin and working the corporate life, had a sideline gig organising small trips back to his homeland - this was his real passion. In time Amanda would be vindicated and Morocco would not be the only Rogue Expeditions running adventure on the African continent. But before we get to that let's go check on the moment domino number two began to fall.

Back on the roads of Austin with the winds of the first ever Morocco trip in her sails, Allison was crunching out her second run of the day, the so-called afternoon double in Rogue Running parlance, with her Rogue Athletic Club pro colleagues. Running 100 miles a week together gives great time to exchange ideas and muse on topics. Any runner will tell you that the mind can be cleared whilst running. Pre-run the mind can race with anxiety loops and worries that then evaporate and new positive thoughts emerge during the run. Usually these new thoughts are more creative thoughts, more forward thinking, more progressive. Some runners even dictate notes to their phone lest they forget the moment. A bit like that last thought before you fall asleep at night. That sneaky burst of creative thought that bubbles into existence just before you leave the conscious realm for the night. Either seize it, grab a pen and paper, and scrawl it onto a bedside piece of paper, or let it go, possibly forevermore. These running thought bubbles are somewhat like that, ephemeral and elusive, enchanting and fleeting. Yet many runners use this altered brain state during a run as a part of their general process. A way to unblock thoughts or get a different perspective. Something akin to a meditation whilst in motion. Whilst the body is firing signals at you about how tired your legs are, or how much your lungs are burning, or how your heart is trying to beat an escape through your ribcage, the brain becomes a more available venue for a useful or creative thought to mosey on into the party. Suddenly it is there, competing with your thoughts of lactic acid in your calf muscles. Jostling against your urge to look at your watch to see how close to the next mile you are. Running provides a cauldron of ideation.

The feeling coming out of Morocco was this was too good for it to be a one-off. But there was no clear plan or goal in mind about what to do next. They talked with Hamid about coming back again the following year, maybe even for two groups back-to-back given the demand. But that was next year and it was just yet the springtime of 2013. These thoughts would have been rumbling around in Allison's mind during the afternoon double. What to do with the momentum from that first trip? A little ripple was going through their close-knit Austin running community. There was positive energy radiating out from the 22 runners who came back with rave reviews, amazing pictures, and stories of a lifetime. Even if some of the stories centred on Ouagadougou. Everything is funny eventually, right? The trip had been an idea to do something fun for Rogue Running. But there was something more there. Some bigger potential. It wasn't just a running trip. Allison and Gabe could both feel it at that point even if they couldn't quite put their finger on it and define it. They hadn't yet minted the new website and written the blurb but thoughts were percolating to that effect.

Matching Allison stride for stride during that afternoon double run was her friend and fellow elite athlete Nicole. Nicole provided the lay-up for the next step.

"My parents have a cabin at Lake Tahoe. You guys should really check it out. I love the trails there. Some of the best trail running I've ever done. Beautiful forest... mountains all around the lake... the beautiful blue water. It's pretty sweet. Maybe you could do a trail running trip?"

We can't know verbatim how Nicole laid out her idea that day, but we can surmise it was pretty straight to the point and economical with words. You can't be too long winded when you're cruising along running sub-7-minute miles through the afternoon heat in Austin. Whatever she said, that crucial next domino fell and a plan was quickly forged. Allison synced up with Erik, another teammate who at the time was also the trail running coach at Rogue Running. Erik was called into action for two reasons. One - he was an expert trail runner and Allison was definitely not, and two - Gabe had blown his holiday days for the year with the Morocco trip and so wouldn't be able to help out on this one.

Gabe, now back at the coalface in the construction world, was no doubt wrestling with similar thoughts to Allison and wondering how to harness the energy emanating from their Morocco trip. These thoughts usually came to the fore for him on the weekends when he would sync up with his old college buddies for some adventure recreation. Gabe's idea of recreation usually involved high speed downhill mountain biking somewhere like Grand Junction, Colorado or Angel Fire, New Mexico. He and his buddies would grind up climber trails through the dust and the scrub, to hit the start points for the sweetest and flowiest trails to thunder down. Downhill mountain biking is usually a question of finding that sweet spot of being *just* in control, but knowing you're almost losing it. Usually you know someone who has reached this point as they will have a very silly grin plastered across their face that they can't seem to wipe off. The grin wearer is engrossed in maneuvering their body and slaloming the bike through turns to maintain momentum at all costs. Hitting jumps at the right speed to clear them smoothly but not over-rotate and disappear out over handlebars. Similar to running this mountain biking platform pretty much clears the mind of all other thoughts. We often call this flow. Runners, mountain bikers, gamers, gardeners, writers, artists, Buddhist monks, fighter pilots, matadors, wingsuiters, all know this phenomenon. Most of our lives our mind is an unruly kaleidoscope of thoughts smashing against each other all the day long trying to keep your attention. Breaking out of this cycle through your favourite pastime is something humans have been doing for a long time. We've probably eaten every plant and fungus in all the ancient forests throughout all of human time trying to access a form of this mind state.

On one of these days out Gabe and his buddies were riffing on one of their favourite topics - business ideas. How to come up with the killer idea to make a million. How to escape the corporate life of 'working for the man' by coming up with your own idea, your own company. They would circle up the bikes at the top of a climber trail, huffing and puffing, wiping sweat out of eyes, and adjusting bike saddles for the switch to downhill mode. In these interstitials the business ideas would be pitched up and tossed out in rapid succession. From the obscure to the ridiculous they just didn't seem to land on anything that really fizzed. On one of these rides a buddy of Gabe's shot down yet another business plan but followed up with encouragement.

"I think you've already got your idea Gabe. Curated running vacations. You guys already created it." They all ripped into the next downhill in a cloud of dust, a squeal of brakes, and a few whoops. A seed was germinating.

Before we take off with Allison to Tahoe an obvious question at this point is - what is the difference between trail running and regular road running? How could a semi-professional runner like Allison who was competing at an elite level not be qualified to run on a different surface? Well, the difference to some in the running community is big. The reality is that it is still just putting one foot one in front of the other, over and over again. We can generalise a few key differences though. Trail running generally involves some amount of navigational skills, an ability to read maps, interpret terrain, etc. Road running by comparison is generally following street signs and typically a little more in straight lines. Trails are often leading to places of beauty in the natural world, through forests, to lakes, up to mountain peaks, around valleys, and across open plains. So by their nature the trails underfoot vary, from rocks and pebbles, dirt and sand, mud and grass, pine needles and bare rocks. Pavement is pretty much pavement wherever you pound it. Whilst out on trails you may be required to look after yourself a little more, basic first aid is useful, a communication plan if something goes wrong when out of cell service. Road running more often takes places where there are other runners around and there is a safety net of a passing car in case of an accident or illness. The consistency underfoot of road running generally allows you to cruise along faster than trail running. And trail running generally involves more time going up and down hills or even mountains, making it generally slower.

One of the sneaky little secrets of trail running in the mountain context is that it involves quite a bit of hiking. Road runners often dislike this fact and prefer to be able to monitor consistent pace per mile and discern pace improvement more easily. Trail runners often rebuke this fascination with speed and distance covered and say that the undulations of the terrain coupled with changes between running and hiking mean it is better overall for our bodies from a physiological standpoint. We could go further down the rabbit hole here, but let's just agree we can see that there are differences and we will leave it to the runners of the world to figure out if they matter, or God forbid, decide which is better or worse!

"To be honest, I knew nothing about trail running," states Allison with total honesty reflecting on this first Tahoe trip idea. She is being, as is her general style, somewhat self-deprecating here. As of Spring 2013 her total trail running experience amounted to just one run on trails - but that run was 50 miles long! It had been the previous summer of 2012 when on a whim she decided to join a couple of friends who were heading up to the small mountain town of Leadville, Colorado to participate in the Leadville Endurance Run. Leadville, especially its banner distance race which is 100 miles long, is a race etched into the history of trail running and ultra running - 'ultra' in this context meaning any distance beyond a traditional 26 mile marathon. If you think running 50 miles through the Rocky Mountains of Colorado on your first ever trail run is a bit excessive, you'd be exactly right. This isn't normal. But this is what you can do when you're an elite athlete. Allison even placed top ten in the race which gave her the confidence to go for 100 miles the following year - but that race wouldn't take place until after the Tahoe trip. So, Erik's help and experience with the nuances of trail running would be important.

Allison and two friends taking a break during the Leadville 50 in 2012 - her first trail run ever

* * *

"This is the life I want to lead."

ALLISON

July 2013

With Erik's help they quickly filled the 8 available spots for the Tahoe running trip from the pool of athletes he was coaching at Rogue Running. It was pitched to the trail runners as a fun running camp in a beautiful place with guided runs, accommodation and food all included. They would call this experience 'Run Tahoe' starting a trend of trip naming that would see 'Running Trip to Morocco' jettisoned and replaced by 'Run Morocco' and a precedent set for all future trips as yet unconceived. The trip would be very different from Morocco, but the essence would be the same. It wouldn't have the cultural allure and exoticism of a trip running in the Sahara, but it would offer a great way to beat the summer heat of Texas whilst exploring a beautiful part of the US. The runners would be guaranteed great running routes, great food, mountain ambience, lake swims, zero stress, and guides would take care of anything that might arise.

Allison, Erik and Erik's then-wife Ashley flew up to California in July just a couple of days ahead of the group. Allison's training partner Nicole had provided them with a bunch of trail recommendations and they hammered through 5 runs in 2 days in order to get their bearings on the trails. They stocked up Nicole's family cabin with a long weekend's worth of group food and wine and headed to the Sacramento airport with a passenger van to pick up their trail runners. What followed turned out to be part summer camp, part trail running training camp, and part forest retreat. By Allison's admission they were pretty much winging it and figuring it out as they went along but Nicole had come up trumps with both her cabin and her trail recommendations.

Lake Tahoe, perched over 6000ft above sea level amidst the Sierra Nevada mountains and straddling the state line of California and Nevada, is one of the jewels of the United States. The lake's clean, clear water covers a spectrum of blues from deepest dark inky depths in the centre, to almost Caribbean-looking azures near its edge of rocky shores and sandy beaches. The lake, a pleasing oval shape with 71 miles of shoreline, sits in a vast basin ringed by mountain peaks which rise from the shore to over 9000ft with their flanks cloaked in pine forest all the way to the water's edge. The trails around Tahoe, some of which are world famous such as the Tahoe Rim Trail and the Pacific Crest Trail, offer beauty around every corner for the would-be trail runner. Powdery dry single track trails contour through forests filled the smell of the pine needles. Trails punch through forest clearings offering opportunity to view the wildflowers which run rampant in the summer window between heavy winter snows that cloak the ground much of the year. Viewpoints along the trails offer glimpses above the timberline to the grey peaks of the Sierra Nevada above. The simple colour palette remains unchanged much of the summer - vivid clear blue skies above, stark grey naked mountains next, then a swathe of dark green forest, and of course the lake itself, deep and rich and blue. Something about these greens and blues in particular of forest and water, feed the soul and call us back to nature. These colours assure us of security and sanctuary in some deeply rooted instinctive way. It can be fun to venture above the treeline into the high alpine rocks offering the best vantage points over the lake. But the return to the trees and shoreline is always somehow a relief.

There are many ways to enjoy Lake Tahoe and many thousands of Americans visit it every summer to hit the beaches, kayak or paddleboard, boat around the lake, or perhaps bike along its edge. No doubt these are all highly enjoyable outings. But the beauty of trail running at Tahoe, especially if you can spare a few days, is the opportunity to see it from above, from a range of different aspects. Up in the forest the views just keep coming. Framed by mountains in the background, pine trees and flowers in the foreground, your phone just keeps on coming out of your pocket for another picture. There is of course the functional advantage of being able to cover a lot of ground quickly by running instead of hiking. Add in the inevitable endorphin release during and after each run, and it is fair to conclude that running the Tahoe trails is a deeply enjoyable experience.

Sharing the cabin together, even if it meant bunk beds and a few people to a room, added an intimacy and summer camp vibe to the experience for the group of runners. The group mingled and interacted in a way that is lost when staying at a hotel with private rooms. Rather than retire to private space in the afternoons after runs they stayed in the communal areas and the conversations never stopped. The group came into the trip knowing each other to some degree as they all shared Rogue Running in general. But the Run Tahoe trip afforded them the time and space to check out of normal life, participate in a shared experience, exchange ideas and stories, and really get to know each other. Somehow this can be lost when on a family trip or even a trip with close friends. There is something unique about spending time getting to know relatively new people. It puts you into modes of conversation that we don't use every day. The guide team of Allison, Ashley and Erik, worked to shuttle everyone to and from the trailheads, guide the runs, and prepare breakfast, lunch and dinner every day. That left plenty of time and brain energy to focus on having great conversations with others in the group or some time alone with your thoughts. The runners may have sold the trip to themselves as an escape from the Texas heat, a break from their normal routine, or even a training block to get some great runs in, but there was more to it than just running. The daily running is a big component of course, it is what all the participants love to do. It was the minimum everyone in the group had in common and, as previously mentioned, it generally puts runners in a good headspace for the rest of the day. But perhaps the real magic of the experience is not necessarily the miles run, but the meandering dinner conversations, or the evening breakout sessions over a glass of wine by the firepit - the connections forged and moments of understanding gained. There is a reason that Fortune 500 companies spend, pardon the pun, a fortune trying to engineer and design these moments with the corporate retreats and 'management off-sites.'

Long run smiles during the inaugural Run Tahoe trip

One of the people most benefitting from the checkout from normal life and Texas summer heat was Allison herself. Experiencing a feeling bearing uncanny familiarity to a certain moment of clarity the year before, thousands of miles away in the Moroccan Sahara, she found herself on the phone to Gabe. She stood on the deck of the cabin gazing out through the sea of pine trees around her, insects chirping the evening away all through the forest. Inside the post-dinner conversation bubbled, punctuated now and again with explosions of laughter. She clutched the stem of a wine glass in one hand and pressed her phone to her ear with the other. Gabe, back in Texas, probably had concrete pours and contract deadlines on his mind, but he listened patiently as Allison tried to unpack the epiphany she was having in the forest.

"This is the life I want to live," she found herself saying, not usually disposed to such moments of profundity. "I don't want to be in the city anymore, working week after week and month after month in the nine-to-five routine. I want to be out here, in the mountains, in the trees, all the time."

We could forgive Gabe an eye roll at the other end of the phone and this moment. We shall never know. Wine and nature were at work on Allison again, yet on some level he was in total agreement, and the months and years ahead would bear this out. This conversation was part of their process at that moment of grappling with the idea of a lifestyle change. Their close friends Joel and Nikki had recently sold their house and worldly possessions, bought a RV, and driven off into the mountains of New Mexico to lead their new life. Allison and Gabe were jealous - why didn't they do that? Lead a different life, change the path they were on, head off into the Great American West.

Organising these trips to Morocco and now Tahoe had afforded them the pause from the noise of daily life they needed in order to glimpse what they wanted. The aggregate experience of those 2013 Morocco and Tahoe trips would equip them with both the vision of the life they wanted plus the confidence and conviction to pursue it. Their course was set during this period even if they didn't know exactly what the destination looked like. Typically in life we are guided by gut, by intuition, along a path without having a map of the terrain ahead. They weren't able at this point to lay out the exact plan for their business as it would unfold. There was no precise strategy but the raw material was already in their minds. Over the next few years they would lead the life of small business owners building their dream. Scrapping and fighting to make their ideas a reality and their business work. Looking back, they can now reflect that they alternated between 'this is the best idea ever, we love our lives' and 'what in the fuck are we doing?' Often those swings happened on an hourly basis during a typical office day ensconced in front of their MacBooks.

Much like the inaugural Morocco trip, the first Tahoe trip in 2013 came about organically and was the beta edition for something more concrete. It would become the domestic summer getaway, sitting alongside trips to more exotic foreign destinations. Gabe missed the first edition but would come to take ownership of these domestic trips and sculpt them and form them into dream getaways. The first trips are exciting and new and shiny. But for the tour guide the joy of repetition is the feeling of assuredness, of being embedded in a place and its stories. As one becomes familiar with a place one can interpret that place better for the visitor, unpack its history, understand the why of a place, answer questions before they even form in the mind of the visitor. For Gabe and Allison these feelings and moments were ahead. 2013 was the year things began, 2014 would be the year things would never turn back.

On the theme of never turning back, Allison had the small detail of a 100 mile long run to attend to after the Run Tahoe trip. With plenty of trail miles in her legs out west at Tahoe, she headed to Leadville again probably feeling more confident and ready than the previous year. The distance was twice as long, but she would discover that the effort and pain required was not double - it was more like exponentially more. An elite road marathoner like Allison running a 100 mile mountain run is a bit like taking a Formula 1 race car and putting it into a World Rally Championship stage. It probably isn't ideally suited, but it is still a powerful machine and will get around the course somehow, maybe sustaining a few dings in the process. That analogy pretty much sums up Allison's second Leadville experience. She finished. But pretty it was not. She got it done. It took almost 30 hours of forward progress to complete those 100 miles. A glimpse into the pain and resolve required to do so is provided by Gabe. He joined Allison late in the race as a pacer. Pacers join the racers to coach them, cajole them, berate them, bribe them with snacks, force them to drink water, maybe lie to them occasionally. Just do whatever it takes to continue the forward progress. Somewhere late in the race, late into the night, and high in the thin air of the Rocky Mountains, Gabe plodded along, his headlight illuminating his little part of Colorado, as he followed Allison's bobbing field of light just head, as they climbed switchback after switchback up a mountain pass. The miles were not flying by.

"You're doing great! Almost to the top now! Last switchback!" He tried the cajole tactic again, mixed lightly with lying.

"HOW THE FUCK DO YOU KNOW?!" came the volley back at him through the mountain air. Yikes. Wrong tactic. Maybe silence and solidarity is the better strategy for this moment. Gabe swears he has never before or since heard an outburst of vitriol like this from his dearest wife. The things 100 miles will do to you, huh?

| 4 |

Falling Into Place: Kenya

*"When you meet the right people, you feel so much at
ease. You think - this could work."*

KINUTHIA

Why Kenya? You'd be entitled to ask. First Morocco, then
Tahoe, why was Kenya the next trip to be added? There is
something about the power of a direct introduction from someone
whose judgement you trust. Amanda had joined the trusted network on the Morocco trip. She vouched for Kinuthia and vouched
for Kenya, tipping her domino into the game. She felt Allison and
Gabe really should meet him. She stayed in touch with Kinuthia after her trip to Kenya with him. Kinuthia describes his trips as,
"small groups, forming strong bonds and friendships," such that
they stay in touch and continue to see each other when back in the
US. This concept and this introduction resonated.

As we've seen in the previous chapter, 2013 was a time of grappling for purchase for our would-be entrepreneurs. Grappling with their idea, trying to define it, get it into clearer resolution, trying to take a fuzzy collection of thoughts and polish it up into a refined concept. The idea of selling running trips was for now sort of an amorphous blob moving forward under its own momentum. They could feel this thing moving and were deciding just how on board they were, and where it was all going. With the first Run Tahoe trip they had baptised a few more evangelicals and released them back into the wild of the Austin running world to spread the good word. Interest was growing. There was such strong demand for the next Morocco trip that they opted to add two trips rather than one for Spring 2014. They promised another Run Tahoe trip for Summer 2014. But maybe even that wasn't enough. Why not another location? What harm in following Amanda's hunch? It is hard in hindsight to gauge the level of commitment to the Kenya idea before they met Kinuthia and saw the gleam in his eyes. But after a couple of beers shared in downtown Austin at the Yellow Jacket Social Club it was clear that the amorphous blob was heading for Kenya.

When I ask them about it, Allison and Gabe reflect on those first introductory beers with Kinuthia decisively - "we jived, the energy was right." Once again, like with a certain Moroccan tour guide, the gut feeling was good. We humans like to think we are in control and making logical decisions during our lives. We imagine thoughtfully weighing up pros and cons, making balanced, informed choices. But so much of our decision making is actually on autopilot. Within seconds of meeting new people we pick up on signals that we cannot translate into language. It is like our brains are running algorithms that we have no insight into. When I asked Kinuthia about his memory of the same meeting he says, "when you meet the right people, you feel so much at ease, you think - this could work." Put another way, Allison tells me, "when you know, you know."

Kinuthia had moved over to Austin several years before and was grinding away in the corporate world with AT&T. His passion though was organising small scale trips back home to Kenya. Curating an experience of his culture and homeland for his clients. His eyes lit up on this topic, it was clear where his passion lay. His ever-present broad smile broadened brilliantly a little more. He had no background whatsoever in running, but he was prepared to entertain the idea of a running trip. Kenya has roads, Kenya has runners, why not? During those beers with Allison and Gabe he was probably already moving around the pieces in his mind - places they could stay, fitting in the typical Maasai Mara safari experience around days which offered running, a visit to Iten - home to Kenya's greatest runners. He possibly had a mental image of an American runner fleeing from a disgruntled Cape Buffalo (consistently Africa's most dangerous animal despite esteemed colleagues who have more teeth) - if so, he kept that to himself. Kenya was a go for development and they embarked on the planning process - a year of back and forth email tennis, countless phone calls, continual iterations to the itinerary, and a scouting trip to lay the key groundwork.

Kinuthia, Melly, Allison & George during the initial Run Kenya scouting trip in 2013

They launched the trip with another info session held at the Rogue Running training room. A chance for potentially interested runners to ask questions, field concerns, meet the guides, and get their own gut feeling. This would be Allison and Gabe's first experience of dealing with one of the realities of international tourism - that there is always a crisis or concern around the corner. On 21st September 2013 four armed gunmen from the terrorist group Al-Shabaab burst into the Westgate shopping mall in Nairobi. The attack was characterised as a retaliation for Kenyan military intervention in Somalia. By the end of the day, 71 were dead and over 200 injured. The attack was a huge blow to Kenya's reputation in the tourism sector. Kenya's economy is heavily reliant on relatively big-spending safari tourists all transiting through Nairobi. Allison and Gabe learned that to offer international travel experiences, they would have to become versed in geopolitics, stay tuned to natural disasters, become meteorologists everywhere they operated, monitor currency fluctuations, and generally become attuned to existential threats to their trips that lurked unseen around the corner. As trips were added in the years ahead, complexity grew, and potential for something to go wrong increased. Back at that moment the response of Kenyan government seemed swift and assured, Kinuthia gave them the green light to press ahead, and their runners were not dissuaded by the news headlines - Run Kenya was quickly sold out.

* * *

"Gabe, you should come take a look at this. There has been an... incident."

AMANDA

November 2014

A little over twelve months after sitting down for those beers in Austin, Allison, Gabe and Kinuthia were together in Nairobi awaiting the arrival of their group of runners. Joining them was Kinuthia's right hand man and key lynchpin of the trip, George. Kinuthia might not have been a runner but George certainly was. Not only a good runner himself George was plugged into the local running scene in Kenya and helped a group of up-and-comer athletes trying to make it to the bigtime. He was also involved in a local organisation Kabete Cares which focused on engaging street kids with team sports. George radiated good energy - he embraced the Rogue Expeditions concept and quickly became the day to day driving force of the trip on the ground.

The whole team had spent a busy few days putting the finishing touches and details to what they hoped would be an unforgettable twelve days exploring Kenya through the medium of running. Most of the group of runners arrived in Nairobi just before midnight and quickly hit the hay for the night after a long pull from the US. Next morning bleary eyed runners emerged from hotel rooms for what was advertised as a nice shakeout run to get in the groove and wake up the legs after all those hours on an airplane the previous day. The weather that morning was finally clear after a week of storms - heavy rains had churned the dirt roads on the outskirts of Nairobi into a sticky, dark red, paste. One of the runners, Mark, promptly and dramatically tumbled across the breakfast area of the hotel in the process of trying to fill a water bottle from a dispenser. A three inch step in the middle of the dining area was the culprit and a quickly ballooning ankle was the result. Purples and blues quickly inked their way around Mark's growing ankle as the hotel team offered a few ice cubes with a smile. Back to bed you might reason, prop that ankle up and recover for the rest of the trip. Not so for Mark. He decided he had come a long way for this running trip and with the spirit of injured runners everywhere, decided to give it a go as he hopalonged his way to join the rest of the group.

The group huddled outside the hotel in their coats in the cool damp morning air whilst Allison and Gabe tried to transmit some enthusiasm and a few directional pointers for the run awaiting them. They headed off running a mile or so to the Karura Forest, a magnificent patch of old growth forest right on the outskirts of northern Nairobi, bordered by neighbourhoods containing many of

Kenya's international embassies. They splashed through puddles on streets flanked by imposing high walls, the tops fortified with razor wire, and punctuated occasionally with important looking entrances. After a mile it was clear Mark was really injured and he opted to wait by the trailhead rather than run further into the forest itself. The group streamed off into the towering trees and got into the groove of the running only to find that with every few steps a brick was forming on the sole of each shoe. The mud was churning up into a decidedly determined adhesive. They slopped along, slippin' and a-slidin', and making the most of what is an astonishing piece of remnant forest which stands steadfast against the encroaching urban sprawl beyond. The Karura has a doggedly determined community of friends which since 1932 have fought to save the urban forest from development threats and maintain the astonishing array of biodiversity hiding in its thousand or so hectares. The group discovered beautiful waterfalls and monkeys swinging in the treetops as they explored the muddy trails of the Karura.

Mark meanwhile decided to use this spare time to clear the newly formed clay bricks from the bottom of his shoes. He hopped his way to a concrete drainage culvert at the side of the street. The culvert ran swiftly with gurgling muddy storm waters - a little too swiftly in fact. No sooner had Mark dipped his shoe into the stream to remove some mud, than the shoe set sail on the current. The newly launched Nike yacht sped off along the street with Mark hopping determinedly after it, intently focused on not letting it out of his sight. Little did Mark know that the shoe had charted a course straight into restricted embassy grounds. He was approaching an armed embassy entrance. There were in fact two armed guards, assault rifles slung across their chests, having their dreary morning interrupted by a large foreign man, with a strange lopsided gait, apparently wearing only one shoe, looking distressed, gaining speed and heading straight towards them. The guards straightened slightly, their training automatically moved their trigger fingers to the ready position. In the next crucial few moments they followed the path of Mark's determined eyes to the shoe bobbing along in the culvert. One of the guards swiftly stooped and retrieved the shoe from the water and smiles were exchanged all around.

All smiles on sloppy, slippery Nairobi trails

Later back at the hotel, Mark reunited with his soggy shoe and a soggy group of runners, a welcome *karibu* feast was being laid out for the runners. Tables were being prepared to receive mounds of vegetables accompanied by platters of roasted meats, and Kinuthia was aiming to stave off afternoon post-run jetlag with a quick pre-dinner lecture on the history, geography and culture of the areas they would see in the coming days. Allison and Gabe meanwhile were plotting a plan to get Mark an x-ray on his worsening ankle.

Before they could solve this first medical incident, however, they were interrupted by another runner, Amanda, arriving and rather calmly delivering a quite urgent request.

"Gabe, you should come and take a look at this. There has been an incident."

The incident turned out to be Amanda's roommate Yvette (who we've already met during a taxi ride from Marrakech through Atlas Mountains), fresh out of the shower, looking sheepish, and wrapped up in a towel with blood seeping through said towel and shattered glass strewn all over the bathroom. It transpired that the Karura mud had struck again as Yvette slipped during her post-run rinse off and collided with the shower. The glass door was somewhat shatterproof - it was held together by embedded chicken wire style mesh which prevented it going into a million pieces, instead it went into maybe a thousand. Thankfully, closer examination de-escalated the situation. Amanda was a nurse and assessed that none of the cuts were serious and even generously volunteered to apply bandages to patch Yvette back together again. Mark got his x-ray at a local hospital and had his fracture worries downgraded to a sprain, which put him out of commission for a couple of days, but at least leaving him with some hope of running later in the trip if things progressed well. We can spare a moment at this point for Allison and Gabe who must have snuck away for a moment, exhaled deeply, met eyes, raised eyebrows, and thought - wow, Day 1, we haven't even left Nairobi yet. What else can possibly go wrong in the twelve days of crisscrossing Kenya ahead?

* * *

"Wow. I have never seen a river here before!"

MELLY

The itinerary ahead was ambitious and varied. First the group struck off north from Nairobi spending a day in the green expanses of Mount Kenya National Park and the following day in another national park at Lake Nakuru - home to more flamingos than you can possibly imagine. They continued the northward meander with a day spent near Nyahururu, the town home to the impressive Thomson's Falls. The name Nyahururu probably comes from the *Maa* (language of the *Maasai* people) word *e-naiwurruwurr* which approximately means waterfall. In the late 19th century a Scotsman named Thomson 'found' (it wasn't lost) the impressive 240ft waterfall for which the town is known and promptly named it after himself, as the British explorers of the era were wont to do. The same Scotsman was one of the early colonist explorers attributed with the naming of the country of Kenya at large. Local names for Mount Kenya, such an important and iconic centre point on the landscape rising above the plains all around, sounded something like Kenya to the ears of European visitors, and so the area began to be marked Kenia or Kenya on maps. The original names for the mountain are varyingly reported as something like *"Kĩĩma- Kĩĩnyaa"* or *"Kĩ-Nyaa."* These local names describe the mountain's stripes of black rock and white snow - some accounts even suggest they may compare the mountain's colours to those of an ostriches' feathers! One can make sense of many of the names of Kenya's towns, mountains and other geographic features by trying to unravel the imperfect anglicization of words from local languages, of which there were and still are many.

The northward travel was aimed at reaching a key destination and core component of the overall itinerary - Iten, Home of Champions. Iten is a running sanctuary perched just over 8000 ft high above the Great Rift Valley. The Great Rift Valley is a colossal geological gash stretching almost 4000 miles from Lebanon to Mozambique threatening to tear Africa in two (it probably will achieve this in another 10 million years or so). It is defined by great sunken trenches, often filled with some of Africa's great lakes, and also huge, raised plateaus and mountains on either side of the rift. Iten, an agricultural village that looks not very different from many other villages in rural Kenya, stands high on one such uplifted area along the rift. Round *Boma* mud huts with thatched roofs sit amongst gardens which spill out to the edge of the rift offering huge views over the landscape. Weathered, wooden picket fences line the red clay roads. The village may not look different, but it is in fact very different. It is the engine room of Kenyan distance running. From this quaint rural setting Kenyan runners go forth to dominate the world of distance running, always jostling for supremacy against their Ethiopian, Ugandan and Eritrean neighbours. Some of the greatest and fastest runners in history honed their skills on the dusty roads around Iten. Ever since the founding of a school by an Irish missionary Brother Colm O'Connell the village has consistently been producing world class athletes. Brother O'Connell had arrived in the village in the 1970s with no background in running and little intention of a long term stay in the area. He began to encourage and coach the local runners at the school and a phenomenon followed. Brother O'Connell still lives in Iten at the time of writing and is sometimes referred to as 'the Godfather of Kenyan Running'. His former pupils include Wilson Kipseng (former world record marathon holder), Florence Kiplagat (former world record half marathon holder) and current greats like David Rudisha (2x Olympic Gold medal and world record holder at 800m). The list of medals, race wins, and records at every running distance, emanating from the village alumni over the years is simply astonishing. For an adventure travel running trip to Kenya, it is simply a must. For the visitor to Iten the first thing to do is to take a picture below the famous red arch over the road into town which bears the town motto; Home of Champions. The next sight to see is, well...there aren't really any other sights to see. The reason to visit is not to see, but to run.

To run in Iten one must appreciate the ritualistic schedule of the running day. At dawn, against a backdrop of cockerels crowing and village life stirring from slumber, hundreds of runners tumble out simple spartan dormitories for a light breakfast - usually a cup of milky tea and a slice of white toast. With the sun starting to lighten the sky they are quickly underway streaming out in groups onto the dusty, dark-red, dirt roads around the village. The runners hammer off at incredible speeds whilst the local farmers herd groups of goats and cows out to pasture at a more sedate pace. Even the slowest runners here could win your local small town marathon anywhere else in the world. Nowadays the runners come here from all over the country for a chance at winning the running lottery. Just to secure a place at one of the training camps in the village - many now managed by former champions - is an achievement. Many runners will have spent all the money they have to secure a spot in the basic dormitories and mingle in the running scene. They hope to catch the eye of the local coaches and talent spotters who might buy them a ticket to the big time. A chance to race overseas in Europe perhaps or the Middle East. Somewhere there is prize money on offer. Running in Iten is what soccer is to the starry-eyed boy kicking a patched-up football in the favelas of Rio de Janeiro. A way out. A way to secure another future. Support a family. Thoughts of glory and medals are much farther down the pecking order of priorities initially.

When visiting Iten during their scouting trip with Kinuthia and George, Allison and Gabe were irrevocably impacted by Iten. It brought home the realities of running in such a visceral way. The global industry that running had become - the merchandise, the technology, the media coverage, the celebrity status of runners - seemed in the same moment bigger than ever and also a little point-less and superfluous. On the scouting visit Kinuthia took them to see a newly completed running track in Iten, made with real rub-berised running track surface rather than the dirt track most of the village used. The new track was for athletes who could pay. George asked if Allison would like to run with him for a lap around the track, to which she replied that she didn't have any running clothes with her. "You need special clothes to run?" George enquired quizzi-cally. Fair point, so she trotted out a lap in hiking pants to appease him. Soon after they spotted none other than Mo Farah trotting out his laps around the shiny new track. Initially he seemed wary of the visitors and stated there was 'no media' allowed. But he relented for a quick snap with George - their picture a wonderful juxtapo-sition of attitudes towards the world of running. With all options at Farah's disposal, any training facility in the world, any coach, any new-fangled shoe or watch or heart monitor to give an edge, any nutrition advice or recovery methods he could think of - he chose Iten. Something about the running community in Iten had an al-most monastic feel. All the noise and frivolities were stripped away. Cranking out miles day after day, finding consistency, keeping up with the person at your shoulder - this was all that mattered. Run-ners, both Kenyan and foreign, came to Iten to find their true run-ning selves, to get back to basics in a Rocky IV sort of way.

Arriving in Iten, Kenya - The Home of Champions

The first ever Rogue Expeditions group to Kenya had found their groove by the time they hit Iten. Much like with the groups in Morocco and Tahoe before, the group dynamic took a day or two to settle in and then it thrived. Bodies became used to the daily routine of cranking out a scenic run after breakfast each morning, and then traveling onwards in the afternoons to see yet more beautiful African landscapes. They had Kinuthia and George providing cultural insight and history facts along the way. They had Allison and Gabe prepping them each day and taking care of all their needs. The group had bonded and gotten to know each other, Yvette's shower injuries were almost healed and hadn't held her back a bit, Mark's ankle was returning to normal size and he was gearing up to join the group for one of the highlight runs of the trip. The storied roads of Iten would be the location for the trip 'long run.' This borrowed from a time-honoured Rogue Running tradition back in Austin where one day every week was a run significantly longer than your typical comfortable daily distance. If you were a 3 miles per day runner it was time to shoot for 7, if you were 7 per day it was time to shoot for a half marathon. Iten offered every conceivable running distance with its maze of roads fanning out in all directions around the village into the agricultural land beyond. Forgiving soft dirt underfoot, gradual rolling terrain, beautiful rural scenes to run through - this was running Mecca. The elevation ensures manageable cool temperatures whilst the thin air would guarantee burning lungs and a pumping heart in that satisfying and challenging sort of way. The Rogue crew would get the opportunity to try and hold pace with some of the local fliers - even if just for a few yards! George had invited local runners to join the Rogue runners on most of the runs so far on the trip. His network of up and coming athletes were only too delighted to join the visiting Americans and give them an insight into the realities of being an aspiring athlete in Kenya, trying to emerge amongst the best in the world, often against the odds. Seeing Iten and running there brought those exchanges and conversations with the local runners home in a visceral way. Running in Iten was, a bit like the Sahara moment for the Morocco crew, an all-sensory moment to really absorb and savour. To exchange smiles and a few words of encouragement from the local runners was invaluable. To witness the primacy of running to this community, the hope and dreams it provided, was unforgettable.

With their long run in the bag in Iten the group turned around and headed south again. A couple of long travel days were scheduled so they could cover the necessary distance to the Maasai Mara whilst resting legs along the way, stopping only at beautiful Lake Elementaita to break up the journey. Mark had gone all or nothing in Iten and came away with 12 unforgettable miles and an ankle that was now larger than ever and looking angry. Otherwise everyone was in great shape and in high spirits and they made their way through increasingly quiet and remote roads into the heart of the Maasai Mara. If you don't know about the Mara, picture a typical safari scene in your mind, or one of those David Attenbrough documentaries with big animals roaming free over vast grassy plains which stretch to the horizon in all directions. Picture tall, elegant, lithe herders with red robes draped around their shoulders, archery bow slung across their back, striding smoothly after a herd of cattle, long wooden sticks occasionally prodding an errant animal at the back of the herd. These are the people of the plains - the Maasai. 'Mara' in their language means 'spotted' and refers to the landscape spotted as it is by occasional trees. This is the natural state of the ecosystem here - vast grasslands with only occasional trees, as opposed to the naturally forested states that make up swathes of the earth. The Mara, along with neighbouring areas of the Serengheti and several other conservation areas, makes up one of the world's most important wildlife sanctuaries. A haven of big animals living free and wild and practically unchanged in millenia - here you can find the infamous 'Big 5' of lion, leopard, cape buffalo, elephant and rhino, as well as hordes of other mighty creatures from your childhood wildlife playset - hyena, cheetah, hippo, crocodile, wildebeest, giraffe, zebra, gazelle, hunting dog and jackal. A cornucopia of wildlife unlike anywhere else in the world.

As many documentaries as you might have watched, no matter how incredibly vivid that Planet Earth and subsequent shows can transport the sights and sounds into your living room, there is simply nothing like being there. Feeling it in an open-sided vehicle. Catching exciting glimpses of elusive and enigmatic creatures living out their daily dramas of life and death. Absorbing the rhythm of passage of a Mara day from sunrise, to sweltering midday heat, to busy sunset hour as the day sweeps across the landscape. It is a cliche, but this time it rings true - there simply is not anywhere else like.

But all that is once you get there. The first ever Rogue Expeditions Kenya crew were deep into a long day of driving. Crankiness levels were variable. They had been jostling and bouncing around on a less than smooth road for several hours. An experience that has come to be described endearingly on Rogue trips as an African Massage - basically getting your spine mashed and stretched and mashed again without end. Then they stopped. The runners stirred at the stoppage, unfolding themselves from a variety of contortions in the vans. They glanced out of one side of the van and then the other. Their glances sought their accommodation, a camp set out in the plains amongst the wildlife action, but none was to be found. Instead, next to them, several Maasai herders with their herds of goats and cows looking out over a river into which the dirt road they were travelling on disappeared.

"Wow," said Melly, one of their minivan drivers, "I've never seen a river here before."

The Rogue convoy disgorged its road weary runners on to the side of the new river to do exactly what the Maasai herders were doing - watch the water flowing by. The herders were using stones to mark the movements of the river at the water's edge. The little line of stones indicated that the river was getting lower. But apparently not low enough to risk herding their valuable livestock into the swift current. The late rainy season October weather had thus far afforded nice temperatures for running and even some pleasantly chilly mornings and evenings for the Rogue crew. At this moment though, when everyone just wanted to get this drive finished and chill at their safari camp accommodation, the rain was far from welcome. For a while everyone shuffled around in boredom until a Land Rover approached the river from the other side. The park ranger driving the Land Rover was apparently feeling a little more gung-ho than everyone on the other side of the river - he didn't seem to be stopping. The crowd on the river bank had somehow been growing in the interim, several kids and a couple of expectant dogs had joined the Rogue runners, the herders, the goats, the cows, and all stood sentinel now on the river bank below a dramatic bruised sky. The 4x4 edged in the river, fast flowing brown water creeping up the bodywork as it inched forward. Quickly the wheels disappeared, then the bumpers were submerged, then the headlights were lost below the flow, the waterline crept up the bonnet onto the windscreen, until finally only part of the roof and the exhaust snorkel could be seen edging through the middle of the river like a hippo in stealth mode. Gradually the Land Rover began to reappear from the murky water again and it lumbered out on the other riverbank triumphant. The Rogue group and the Maasai herders exhaled as one and unclenched their buttocks. The driver opened his door to allow a gush of river water to escape from the cabin, seemingly unperturbed at this slightly sketchy crossing, and then roared off into the darkening Mara evening. Everyone else present decided to do a little more waiting.

Eventually some Land Rovers arrived from the safari camp to help the Rogue crew. By now the river flow was silent and smooth, but even so the large 4x4s did a couple of test crossings without any passengers to check everything was safe to proceed. They ferried the runners over high and dry aboard the high-backed 4x4s and then returned to tow the empty passenger vans across the river and the excitement was over for the evening and the luxury could begin. Anyone who has stayed in these safari 'camps' will know that camp is a pretty misleading word here. Long before 'glamping' emerged as a word, there have been four poster beds in the tents of Kenyan safari camps. The 'tents' of this camp were beautiful elevated wooden cabins with thatched roofs that were tucked away thoughtfully in the shelter of towering trees stretching out to shade the cabins from the worst of the daytime heat. This would be the basecamp for the next couple of days of safari action. Nestled for the night in one of these cabins, fragrant notes of African hardwoods in your nose, night-time insect opera performance continuing insistently outside, one feels a giddy expectation. Knowing that out there in the darkness, there are uncountable animals moving around in fenceless freedom. One truly feels a visitor to another domain. A wild place. It is both an incredible privilege and an awesome thrill.

Joining the local Masai residents and waiting for waters to recede

The group had an early start the next morning - you're on the animals' schedule now - and the safari camp staff roused the sleepy runners with fresh coffee delivered right to their tents - clearly not their first encounter with sleepy Americans. Pangs of sleep deprivation were quickly overridden by the thrills of seeing animal after animal. Herds of zebra, harems of impala, a couple of lion brothers swishing their tails as they chilled under a bush, then rhino, then giraffe - it almost seemed too easy. The experienced and knowledgeable safari drivers consulting a map of intuition in their mind to find the best spots. Seeming to know on which day of the week a certain watering hole might be fruitful. Occasionally a cluster of vehicles was a giveaway of a big sighting but there was plenty of room for everyone to seek out their own special moments and unique sightings. It really is something to feel the hush come over a safari vehicle in the presence of these great animals.

One could be forgiven for imagining that this safari was a fitting way to end the Rogue trip, but they weren't done yet. Instead the group got to admire the Mara from above with a flight departing from the dirt landing strip of Olkiombo Airport and its tiny thatched terminal building. The flight brought views of vast wildebeest herds before flying out of the region and on to Kenya's Indian Ocean coastline and the stunning Diani Beach south of the great port city of Mombasa. From mountain highlands, to the great plains of Africa, Kenya had already offered a phenomenal variety of culture, landscape and beauty. Its coastline, though, holds yet more surprises with white sand beaches, warm turquoise waters, and a feast of seafood to choose from. Running reduced to a minimum with more time devoted to lounging on the beach between the multiple seafood meals per day, a short boat ride on the beautiful water to admire the rich sea life in the warm shallow waters, and some swimming to rejuvenate worked legs and joints.

Only when the finish line was in sight did Allison, Gabe, Kinuthia and George clink beers and toast a job well done. They could feel the good vibes emanating from the group of road weary but experience rich runners. The final night at the beach allowed everyone to pause, exhale, look out at the ocean and reflect on an adventure and a tapestry of memories that they couldn't have imagined beforehand. In such moments it almost becomes difficult to remember the arrival day, or even the first couple of days of the trip. It all seems a blur, both seeming very long and very short at the same moment. During these trips we are so engrossed in the experience as to almost be in a constant state of flow throughout. Senses and soul open at all moments to the events unfolding with each passing moment. The leaders, tour guides, organisers, call them what you will, of such a trip are equally engrossed and consumed. Trying to stay a step ahead and keep the whole process on the rails. Aiming to seamlessly transition from one run to the next, one accommodation to the next, one meal to the next, aiming to pull a series of rabbits out of the hat that keep increasing and growing the experience in a pleasing and surprising narrative. When the guests were tucked up in bed each night Allison, Gabe and the local team huddled to review the day and prepare the next. Moving pieces around the board, tinkering with timelines, and reacting to situations as they evolved. Kinuthia and George's team of drivers and logistics support had proved invaluable and integral. Without the correct local support such trips simply do not happen. Bonds are forged with such trips and the one with Kinuthia and his team was solid and set for the years ahead.

Rested and restored from the beach time, most of the group readied for departure out of Nairobi and the long-haul back home, but there was a small crew staying on for a bolt-on to the trip. Mark and his ankle would have the final say on the trip as this bolt-on was his dream - to climb Mount Kilimanjaro, Africa's highest peak, a breathless 19,341ft summit situated just over the border from Kenya in Northern Tanzania. Mark's ankle had recovered somewhat during the safari in the Mara, and during the final days of the trip he had oscillated between cancelling the mountain expedition and going ahead with it. He re-booked his flights back to the US one evening at significant cost and energy effort on the phone to the airline only to wake the next morning and switch the whole thing back again. Bum ankle or not he was going to give it a shot - it would be a long way to come back to get a second try. It takes five days of arduous trekking to climb on to the roof of Africa. Days of tough slogging from hot and humid tropical forest up to frigid ice-capped barren mountaintop. The local mountain guides coach and cajole visiting hikers with the mantra 'pole, pole' - slowly, slowly. They aim to keep heart rates low and breathing deep and steady. The air gets thinner and the body tires more and more the higher you climb but against all odds Mark got it done. Allison and Gabe also summited the mountain for the first time and found the final day at high altitude tough going even with two good ankles. Mark had fulfilled his dream to cap off his trip. Once back in Austin a few days later he went for another x-ray on his still tender ankle. It might not have been fractured before the mountain, but it sure was now!

Feeling good enough for handstands on the summit of Mt. Kilimanjaro

| 5 |

No Turning Back: Bend

"The great tour of the American West: living, moving, dealing with the RV."

ALLISON

2014 had already been a big year of achievements for Allison and Gabe even before they reached the summit of Mount Kilimanjaro in November. Just before the sellout Kenya trip they had been in Morocco with another big group of runners visiting the Sahara again. Whilst in Morocco they had taken some time with Hamid to scout new parts of the country and plan an all-new itinerary called 'Mountains and Coast.' This trip would feature some beautiful new running routes in the High Atlas Mountains and the lesser known Anti-Atlas Mountains before finishing on the Atlantic coastline. With that new itinerary in hand they had plenty of Morocco ammunition for 2015. Now Kinuthia and George had been ordained as their Kenyan dream team or their 'Hamid in Kenya' and they had discovered a formula whereby they would need a 'Hamid in every location' in order to run trips seamlessly. Earlier in the summer of

2014 they had repeated the Run Tahoe trip to much the same great feedback and enthusiasm as the first time around. They had also added a new domestic US getaway in Bend, Oregon called, you guessed it - Run Bend.

Bend is one of those adventure hub towns that acts like a magnet to outdoor enthusiasts. This is explained by the surrounding forests, mountains and rivers stretching as far as the eye can see, providing a playground for all seasons - trail running, mountain biking, mountaineering, rock climbing, and kayaking in the summer, skiing, snowboarding, snowshoe hiking in the winter. Pick your poison - it was all available in Bend. All seasons, all activities. It also offered a small town friendly laid back vibe and a more than adequate selection of craft breweries, pizza places, and food trucks. If you visit it is hard to see who is doing the work in Bend. Regardless of day of the week or time of day, everyone seems to be out playing in nature. Their vehicles festooned with kayaks, mountain bikes, and paddle boards. Parking lots at popular trailheads are constantly busy. It was a place and a community that fitted neatly alongside the concept of what they had offered with the Run Tahoe trip.

What enabled the addition of the Bend trip was a Rogue Expeditions team that was now fully mobile. At the end of May 2014 Gabe had resigned from his construction job in Austin, whilst Allison had been given the green light to work remotely for Rogue Running, so they packed their worldly belongings (many pairs of running shoes) into a rather large and newly purchased RV, rented out their house in Austin and headed west - in the spirit of the Great American adventure since pioneer times. No more envy of their friends Joel and Nikki - now they could compare RV setups and exchange tips on good places to park for the night and pro-tips on where to empty the black tank (RV talk for the sewage storage - you can't always go in the woods!). Summer 2014 was spent hopscotching across the western states with stops in Wyoming, Montana and Washington, visiting friends, playing in nature, sporadic outbreaks of office productivity in the RV, and eventually extended stays in Oregon and California to deliver the Run Bend and Run Tahoe trips in July. They were doing it, living it. The wine-fuelled dream in the pine trees of a year before was happening. They were in it. They were committed. Committed to both the new nomadic lifestyle and their blossoming business idea. It was just over a year from the first trip to Morocco - the one Gabe described as 'no thought of this being a business' - to them uprooting their lives in Austin and committing to the concept of selling running adventures. This was a pivotal moment. In resigning his construction management job Gabe was giving up the only career he had ever known - a healthy paycheck, health benefits, paid vacation, 401k, security. Allison was unplugging from the Austin running community which had fostered her passion for running into a full-time running focused career. But this was the only way to know if their business idea was just a fun thing to do a couple of times a year or it was scalable. Gabe recalls that, "the options were discussed at length and ultimately we would regret not trying."

Finally joining Nikki and Joel with homes in tow, somewhere in Montana

In making such a commitment many people could become paralysed by the 'ifs, buts, and maybes.' One can imagine a certain kind of vertigo setting in when Gabe left work on the final Friday and realised he had no idea when he would next receive a paycheck. Or when they handed over the keys of their house in Austin and realised they were technically 'of no fixed abode.' Financially speaking for their new business the margins were fairly slim. There was no pot of investment money to start the business with. They were solely reliant on pulling in the next interested runner who would sign up for a trip. Pull in enough interested runners and a trip could cover its hard fixed costs. Pull in one runner more than enough, and the trip could yield a little profit. But exactly what were the hard fixed costs was a bit of a moving target. Any new business owner will know (you may also have experienced this planning your own wedding or even your own holiday) that you don't have all the facts and figures before starting out. You can make your best guesstimate. But that is all it is - an estimate. So, they estimated that by renting out their house they could cover mortgage and property taxes. They estimated that by living in the RV they could minimise personal expenditure. They estimated that although Gabe would no longer have a paycheck, that Allison could continue to win some bread remote working whilst they could add some additional trips and bring Rogue Expeditions up to scale. Hopefully they could bring it to a place where they might be able to both get paid out of it - little did they know that this would take several more years! Back in those days (and still today!) Gabe fiddled endlessly with spreadsheets. "I put things in Excel - that's what I do," he admits to me with a smile. He likes to finetune the formulae, mingle with the macros, interrogate the inputs, frowning and sighing at his screen from time to time. This for him is a sort of meditative mental gymnastics which helps him hover close to a decision. One can never know for sure with calculating a guesstimate. Here and there is a number in a spreadsheet cell that is like a licked finger in the wind. But the process helps balance out one's gut intuition. Rationalisation by row and column rather than by pro and con.

This rationalisation enabled them to take the plunge in early 2014. The only way to really find out if a business idea is viable is to run with it - excuse the pun. The Morocco and Tahoe trips in 2013 had not been focused on generating income - they were more like fun marketing trips for Rogue Running. Those first trips were experiments and proof of concept but now they would have to go for it and see if there was viable business to create. See if Rogue Expeditions could stand on its own feet. Two assets that didn't have to be factored into the spreadsheet reckoning were Allison and Gabe themselves. The skills and ideas they brought to the table. To begin with they didn't hire anyone. They did it all by themselves. So it is worth pausing for a moment to see the skill sets and experiences that were already in play. We can also posit the hypothesis that the business would never have gotten off the ground if they had to 'hire themselves.' In a stroke of 'narrator becomes marriage counsellor mischief' we shall let Allison and Gabe describe each other's strengths and weaknesses - truth litmus test baked into the method. I'll use my perch of third wheel perspective to add some colour to the picture.

Allison tells me that, "the balance, in retrospect, was perfect...most of the time." An endorsement of sorts for the partnership. Gabe is quick to point out with a laugh that "on paper, I'm a terrible running guide, I would never have hired myself" but Allison generously admits to me that Gabe was a legitimate outdoor adventure guide and that she was not at the beginning. So we will start with Gabe. Before Rogue he had been responsible for others in outdoor adventure settings of kayaking, rafting and rock climbing trips. He knew the drill there. He had official training in basic wilderness medicine and first aid, lots of personal outdoor adventure experience, and perhaps most importantly, great situational awareness which was transferable and adaptable. Allison also informs me that Gabe is the "gregarious tour guide" - the conversation starter and the laughter maker. From the perspective of a new group of runners they would see this straight off. Gabe is quick with jokes, warm with introductions, and genuine with get-to-know-you conversation. When you get a fresh group of new runners together in an exciting part of the world it is important to break down the walls of introduction quickly and gel the group. Inappropriate humour and alcohol are two very useful tools - Gabe has been known to deploy both effectively. Allison also highlights Gabe's practical and logistical skills, honed through years in the construction world, of "getting shit done, making the background essential tasks happen, and solving problems on the fly." He was detail orientated and had overcome complicated logistics both in the construction world and in organising trips paddling through the Grand Canyon. A trip such as rafting the Grand Canyon is a ton of planning. You need to be fully equipped for three weeks of off-the-grid living on the river where everything is packed in, and everything is packed out. Stress on *everything*. Gabe has regaled me before with stories of a device he calls 'the groover.' A portable toilet for riverside defecation that holds all contents until the trip ends - thankfully such a device is not forced upon running groups. Compared with these river trips, a running trip supported by capable local partners is relatively straightforward. Allison also points out that Gabe sorts the legal contracts, taxes and finances, and for that she is eternally grateful. Ignorance is bliss on that front. So we have a picture, illustrated by his loving wife, of Gabe Steger - adventure tour guide, logistics manager, contracts lawyer, accountant, master of spreadsheets, and also, critically, official parker of the 36 feet long RV. More on that last accolade to follow.

When Gabe tells me about Allison I might have expected a few wise cracks - he usually has some good ones - but instead there is lots of generous praise for "Speedy Mac" as he calls her on this occasion. As he rightly points Allison is "the real runner." It is important to have a runner for a business centred around running after all. Sure Gabe could knock out some miles also, but Allison is not just any runner, she was and is a homegrown hero in Austin, running at a competitive level, plugged into the running community and media, and having her own almost religious following of fans. She would go on to win the Austin marathon in 2017 and 2018 cementing her status in Austin running folklore. Even in the earlier days of Rogue Expeditions though, she was competing at a high level partaking in the US Olympic Trials Marathon in 2012 and 2016. For perspective here, only 196 women in the United States ran a fast enough marathon in the qualifying years between 2008 and 2012 to compete at the 2012 Olympic Trials - only the top 3 at the Trials would make it to the actual Olympics. Allison came in 45th quickest in just over 2 hours and 40 minutes. Four years later in 2016, 226 women had qualified and Allison finished 22nd in just over 2 hours 42 minutes. This is the uppermost echelon of distance running, the halo of phenomenal athletes just around those very few who go on to compete at the Olympics themselves. Gabe recognizes that this largely provided the initial platform and reach to start selling the trips. It ensured authenticity and a qualified running pedigree in the guiding mix. Gabe is quick to explain for me that this running pedigree is but one part of what Allison brings to the table. As the numbers above illustrate there are hundreds of elite women marathoners in the US but not all of them would qualify to be a good business partner and tour guide. What sets Allison apart, amongst other things, are her marketing and design skills. Equally well versed in graphic design, web design, social media content management, marketing email distribution, digital advert campaigns and targeting - Allison is a one woman marketing and advertising agency. Gabe highlights her ability to pull in the next runner with authentic social media content, the right imagery, the correct tone in the written descriptions of the trips. When a business such as Rogue Expeditions has its shopfront online, as so many do nowadays, to have a certain style and feel and image is everything. A website needs to draw you in and communication needs to be clear. Allison had a way of putting a certain topspin on the marketing content that made it just so. And so we conclude marital counselling with Gabe's painting of his wife Allison Macsas - elite marathoner, social media guru, adobe illustrator ninja, webmaster, digital marketing sniper.

What would it have cost to hire the roles that these two covered in those initial years? Too much probably. This is the beauty of the small start-up - one must be good at wearing different hats, and by extension, one must have many hats to wear!

With hindsight we can note that Gabe came from a big, corporate company with planning processes, specialised departments, and standard operating procedures. Allison on the other hand had been working in a bootstrapping start-up that liked to wing it by nature. This yin and yang of business types may be the essential synergy required in a start-up. You need the zest and verve and recklessness of a start-up flying by the seat of its pants. But at some point you need the balance of 'real business' with planning, organisation, strategy, and solidity. What might seem a culture clash between the two styles is on further viewing an essential duality and push and pull of any business. Lean too far in either direction and you are heading for the rocks. Trouble could come in the form of stagnation and staleness of an overly bureaucratic lumbering corporate animal or the quick firecracker pop and fizzle of many start-ups that are all razzmatazz and no substance. Plot a course between these troublesome waters and you'll be on your way to smoother sailing.

Another duality to reflect upon is the split in running speed in those early days. Allison was the one out front leading the runs and marking the turns in the trail for the clients to follow. She could yoyo back and forward through the group relaying messages and checking in on everyone, and still zip back out in front when required. Gabe might not have the raw speed of his wife, but he is perfectly suited for the role they came to call 'the sweep.' Following at the back of the group of runners. Checking in on anyone struggling a little bit, troubleshooting minor injuries and twinges, communicating and coordinating with their drivers and logistics team, thinking three steps ahead so everything went smoothly. In those early trips especially, before other running guides were brought into the mix, they had it perfectly covered with just the two of them. They naturally fitted the roles that were required. Or as Allison puts it, "we balance rather than butt heads." We can probably add another 'most of the time' here!

Besides the attributes of the founders, another cornerstone for Rogue Expeditions in those early days was the Rogue Running community and family that it emerged from. Allison had been a part of Rogue Running as it fought its way into existence amongst the Austin running scene. She had been a part of countless battle plans and roundtables as the business grew piece by piece, adding more and better coaching, improving their methods, developing their pro athlete roster, bringing in more and more wannabee runners to the family. In her words this was "a full free education in running a small business - some of it learning what not to do!" But lots of it was learning the right things to do - get a quality product to people, build community, create a positive environment, get your hands dirty and hustle, build a base from the grassroots. The Rogue Running family also provided the initial database of interested runners to which Rogue Expeditions could market their ideas. The guinea pigs on which the beta could be tested. The fact that Allison had a prior relationship with many of these runners before they turned up in Morocco or Kenya or Tahoe or Bend was invaluable. They already trusted and respected her as a runner and a coach. The runners had the measure of her character and integrity from following her athletic career through local running media. It is fair to say the Rogue Expeditions bandwagon would not have gotten underway without the inherent skills and attributes of Allison and Gabe, but it is also fair to say that there might never have been a bandwagon without the foundations that Rogue Running and the Austin running community provided.

At the time of writing it is easy to interview Allison and Gabe and look back fondly at those emergent months and years of the business and draw crisp images of how everything fell neatly into place. To really get inside how it felt at the time though is another matter. Despite vague gut feelings of 'doing the right thing' there were no doubt frequent bouts of existential dread for Allison and Gabe. We must conjure the image of the Rogue Expeditions home office setup in the RV. We need to factor in that Allison is probably on the sofa wearing a pair of leg-length compression boots which make mechanical groans and wheezes as they massage aching legs from the half marathon she has run that morning - like most mornings. A cafetiere full of coffee will be within arm's reach, a laptop perched on a cushion on her lap. She stares into an Adobe Illustrator file, panning around, cropping, tweaking, never quite satisfied. Gabe meanwhile has a large glass of iced tea, plenty of ice cubes in his glass (Gabe's travels around the world have involved the pursuit of the perfect glass of iced tea with plenty of ice cubes but somehow home is always best), and he takes the more conventional route of sitting at a small RV table with his laptop. He uses a mouse so he can maneuver around the cells of his Excel spreadsheet better. An email notification hits both their email inboxes at the same time. They are all two of the company employees on the mailing list. A notification pops into the top right hand corner of their screens simultaneously - it is a notification from Squarespace, the payment vendor on their website. It can only be one of two things. Either someone has signed up for a trip. Or someone who was signed up has cancelled. The outcome to moods in the RV between these two possibilities is a yawning chasm. It could be delight, vindication, optimism, positivity - let's go out and get a beer and tacos for lunch! Or it could be slammed laptop lids, frustration, doubt, stress, home cooked beans and rice for lunch. In 2014 they had a grand total of about 50 clients for the year between Morocco, Kenya, Tahoe and Bend. Losing or gaining one was everything. They lived and died in those moments. But they kept plugging away in either outcome. A successful start-up requires that you show up for the daily fight, keep scraping, keep seeing the sunny side, keep on keepin' on.

Of course whilst fighting the good fight getting their start-up off the ground they had an extra layer of difficulty to worry about. Life in an RV. Wasn't that supposed to be a freeing, liberating experience? Well, sometimes it was, but often the reality was plenty of hassle along the way. Starting a business together is a great way to test a relationship to the max. Living together in an RV whilst driving around the US adds an extra squeeze to that stress test. As I get Allison and Gabe to reminisce of those RV days of Summer 2014 I sense some unresolved tension. There are clearly some sore points. Their world was a 20 ft long Ford F250 (a vast contraption in and of itself) to which was connected a 13.5ft tall, 36 foot long trailer. It is not far off driving around in a semi truck. Driving this behemoth requires route planning and careful consideration. "You can't exactly whip a U-turn," Gabe offers. Residential streets are a no-go area, missing a highway turnoff could be an hour added to the journey. Getting fuel can be an ordeal as only certain forecourts are large enough and you might have to wait a half hour for the particular pump you can fit beside to come free. Initially they drove in fear of tree branches, power lines, or hitting road construction where they might have to slalom through traffic cones.

When they were underway, death grip on the steering wheel beginning to loosen, the next challenge would be the navigation. Rolling out through West Texas on their way from Austin to Angel Fire, New Mexico or Grand Junction, Colorado, or wherever the first port of call was, Allison's phone would lose service. Or was it Gabe's phone? I don't want to get involved in this dispute. Gabe admits that, "there were definitely some high stress, tense moments with navigation and directions." A silence falls between them on the recording after this statement. You can imagine it - several hours into a drive through the mind bending boredom of West Texas, energy levels low, a little hungry, a little cranky, fuel gauge dipping below a quarter tank, and they miss an exit for a suitably sized gas station. Well is there another one coming up? Gabe will enquire. Well I don't have any phone signal. Allison will reply with a shrug. Well I've only got another 50 miles or so in the tank, and it is 60 miles to Lubbock. Little moments like this are the tense, fraught reality of the RV dream.

The fun really starts when you reach the RV park however. After a long day of spotty phone signal and navigation errors, hot and bothered, ready for dinner and a strong drink, you roll into an RV park and your spot is a little skinny looking, the turning radius looks a little tight, and there are several guys clutching beers and winding their arms in contradictory directions in the name of helping. Gabe calls these guys "the busybodies" - they are in every RV park in America, desperate to strike up conversations with newcomers. Allison admits with a shudder that, "there may be some PTSD from parking." Gabe cuts over her here to remind her that if he is backing up, and she is behind the rig waving him into position but can't see him in the mirror, then he can't see her. That's how mirrors work. That never happened Allison corrects him. It seems there are different versions of the truth operating in their RV memories. "We're stronger for it," Allison concludes in an act of diplomacy, "compared to many couples we saw parking RVs in RV parks we did pretty well." I for one am fascinated. Watching domestic parking implosions at RV parks sounds like good sport and I intend to try it one day. Even when you finally exhale and unclench those buttocks when the RV is parked, there is still the power to connect, the leveling of the trailer, maybe the sewage black tank to empty, groceries to get, and elusive WiFi to search for. This last point saw Rogue Expeditions managed and grown from coffee shops and public libraries across the western US - often sitting outside pirating a wi-fi signal long after the establishments had closed!

On one particular evening in an RV park in Bend, Oregon, all navigating and parking related hurdles of the day crossed, Allison and Gabe were just finishing plugging in the RV and levelling it and so on. Suddenly there was a loud pop inside the trailer followed by smoke and mystery liquid starting to come out from behind the tv screen. Gabe frantically disconnected everything whilst they reviewed the situation. They then replugged and everything seemed to be ok except some appliances weren't working. That evening as they prepared dinner it seemed to be getting dimmer, so they flicked on a couple more lights in the cabin. Then a couple more. The penny finally dropped. Power was not coming through and they had just run the battery flat. A new converter had to be ordered and would take three days to ship to them. They slumped off to a nearby bar and Allison recalls it as an overwhelming moment. There were now expensive parts to buy and they were losing time that needed to be used scouting trails before an upcoming trip - their first ever Run Bend trip in fact. Many of their electrical appliances might not now work. The RV dream was on shaky ground that evening. A couple of days later, they were out scouting a potential run for the new trip along the beautiful McKenzie River trail when Gabe slipped off his mountain bike and sliced open his leg. They hurriedly stemmed the blood with gauze and tape and rushed to the local RV dealership. Not the emergency room, that could wait - the RV store closed at 5. They picked up their new battery and power converter, blood seeping through Gabe's bandages all the while, store attendant probably thinking 'wow this couple must have had a rough parking fight' before finally getting to the emergency room for 18 stitches in Gabe's leg. There are many more RV stories and hijinks but Allison summarises this time of their life well as "the great tour of the American West, living, moving, dealing with the RV." Besides work they were visiting friends, running, hiking, biking, rafting, climbing, in all kinds of fun and wonderful settings. They clearly look back on these days with fondness - even with a few underlying moments of old anxiety.

With hindsight it seems to me that 2014 was the year of commitment and the leap of faith - in a lifestyle sense and in a business sense. It was also the year of moving forward and reaching out for opportunities in addition to taking the ones that came along. The connections that created the Morocco, Tahoe, and Kenya trips had been highly organic and spontaneous. Those dominoes had all fallen into place as if they were predetermined to do so. But as Allison and Gabe committed to the RV lifestyle and their start-up business in early 2014 they also decided to be more proactive with the next trips they wanted to add. For Bend, they had done the math and sought out the opportunity. The Tahoe trip provided the format - a short five trip requiring less holiday days, easy domestic travel for the still primarily US client base, intimate summer camp vibes, stellar trail running, lots of great food, drinks and laughs. Bend was just the kind of place that would appeal to their mainly Texas clientele who wanted to escape the oven of summer, and just the type of place Allison and Gabe fancied parking the RV for a few weeks. They did search out one other destination back at the beginning of 2014 though, and the RV would have to stay at home (wherever that was) for this one. Remember those zodiacs in the ice?

| 6 |

The Spirit of Adventure: Patagonia

"The word adventure has gotten overused. For me, when everything goes wrong – that's when adventure starts."

YVON CHOUINARD

Run Kenya was a triumphant end to 2014 and Rogue intended to kick off 2015 with another big bang - Run Patagonia. Considered by many as one of the world's greatest adventure hotspots, Patagonia is a destination that undoubtedly stirs the imagination of any traveller. A cursory inspection of the world map is enough to arouse interest in Patagonia. It forms the bottom part of the Americas, jutting towards Antarctica like an outstretched finger. On its flanks three of the world's great oceans collide - the confluence of the Atlantic, Pacific and Southern Oceans ensures turbulent seas and highly variable weather patterns. It contains the southernmost permanently inhabited lands on the planet. The 2 million or so Chileans and Argentinians who call Patagonia home are spread across a region so vast you could drop the state of Texas into it and still add California beside it. This landscape is made up of huge open plains and steppes, stunning jagged mountains of the Southern Andes, pristine ancient forests cloaking countless uninhabited islands, and truly massive glaciers forking off the Southern Patagonian Ice Field. To borrow from Yvon Chouinard, founder of the Patagonia clothing brand, with him talking in the context of why the clothing brand adopted the name Patagonia, he says Patagonia brings up, "romantic visions of glaciers tumbling into fjords, jagged windswept peaks, gauchos and condors" - that about covers it.

For Rogue, it was almost an obvious choice - the ultimate adventure destination. They wanted to go there - that bit was for sure. They figured it would be possible to organise a running trip, but it was going to be the most ambitious and complicated trip yet. Patagonia is a place where if you miss a ferry, the next one might be next week. If the weather is bad, it might stay that way for days. If the store is out of supplies, then it is out, there might not be another store. The rock climbers who descend on Patagonia every year talk about going there for 'the season.' This phrase has built into an understanding that it might take the whole season to do any climbing. For every day of stellar rock climbing in Patagonia there are probably a week of other days shoved deep into a sleeping bag cooking noodles on the camp stove again - whilst the wind threatens to prise your tent from the mountainside.

It was clear then that they would need the right contacts on the ground and, yet again, their network would come into play. Allison had mentioned a desire to visit Patagonia to Kate - one of the runners on the first Tahoe trip back in 2013. Kate connected the dots to a Chilean guide she met on a NOLS course. NOLS is the National Outdoor Leadership School, now a global non-profit organisation specialising in training leadership skills in a wilderness setting. Through Kate's NOLS connection they reached Rodrigo and his nephew Nicolas based in Punta Arenas, Chile - just the guys they needed on the ground in Chile to put together a scouting trip. Prior to the scouting trip Gabe had poured over maps and scoured the web for blogs about trails from runners who had visited the area. This research made it clear an extensive scouting trip was required - online research can only take you so far. They would need to cover a lot of ground - a necessity in a vast region - and get their heads around all the logistical requirements. The scouting trip was arranged for January 2014, over a year before the first trips with runners in March 2015 - this continued a trend that it took about a year from initial scouting to put together the logistics, planning, marketing and promotion strategy for a new trip.

They arrived in Punta Arenas, a scruffy port town in the Chilean far south that always manages to make a bad first impression, to stay with Nicolas and his girlfriend Macarena who made a wonderful first impression. As the 19th century became the 20th, Punta Arenas was an important port - a place of industry and bustle, of wealth and importance. Trading vessels navigating around the Americas invariably favour the sheltered waters of the Strait of Magellan, named after the Portuguese explorer Ferdinand Magellan, to the wilder route around the tip of Cape Horn. Magellan was first to sail the strait from the Atlantic to the Pacific 500 years ago in 1520 and the stretch of water he charted has remained important ever since. When the California gold rush commenced in 1848 railroads had not yet reached the west coast of the US. Sailing via Punta Arenas was the fastest way from Europe to the promised fortunes. It was a boomtime for the town - wealth poured into the region. With the opening of the Panama Canal in 1914 however, Punta Arenas lost its strategic importance and was never quite the same again. In the 21st century the town is the stepping off point for adventure tourists heading onwards to destinations around Southern Patagonia or beyond to Antarctica, as well as the hub for oil and gas exploration in the region. The wealth and importance is a little diminished, but there is still plenty of bustle.

Nicolas and Macarena invited Gabe and Allison into their home and fed and watered them for a couple of days whilst they explored ideas about possible itineraries. Nicolas, in his late thirties at the time, was already experienced at providing logistics for scientific expeditions in the region. A man of many talents - a photographer, an architect, an artist, an ex-pro mountain biker - he was full of creative ideas and was clearly imbued with a passion for the region, especially the wilder corners of Tierra del Fuego where few ventured. He worked in tandem with his uncle Rodrigo, older and even more experienced, and more than a little eccentric. Allison and Gabe already had a feel for Rodrigo through the sheer quantity of exclamation marks that punctuated his impassioned emails. In person, he was as resolute as an exclamation mark on many of his core principles. He was an ardent environmentalist. Abhorring waste and a key figure in pushing the increase of recycling for the local municipality of Magallenas. He was somewhat conflicted by mass tourism to the region. In one moment critical of the waste that visitors generate, in another moment trying to use the platform of tourism to impart some of his ideas. He owned a backpacker hostel that required signing a contract agreeing to its environmental principles when you made a booking - only use organic soap, don't waste food, compost food scraps, reject single use plastic and so on.

Together Rodrigo and Nicolas had the insider knowledge and ideas to steer the scouting process. They correctly foretold how getting good food is difficult away from Punta Arena and Puerto Natales, the only large towns of the region. So they had a solution - bring your own supplies and cook team, lest you eat lamb chops and potatoes every single day. The planning process hit snags around the timings of ferries to Tierra del Fuego. They had another solution - a private boat, normally reserved for scientific expeditions, that could be hired to sail the Strait of Magellan to access some wild uninhabited areas of the Tierra del Fuego archipelago. Accommodation options were hard to find so they produced another solution - a remote rustic farmhouse on the main island of Tierra del Fuego itself that could be privately rented. They knew the ins and outs of visiting Torres del Paine national park itself - the centrepiece attraction for visitors. Knowing how best to navigate it's in-demand *refugios* (essentially backpacker style mountain lodges inside the park only accessible by hiking trails) and which trails were more and less trafficked by hikers. Ideas sketched out and a draft itinerary in mind, Allison and Gabe set off to get into the landscape and put theory into practise. The learnings ahead, in both the scouting trip and the actual trips to come, could be shortly summarised as: weather rules everything in Patagonia and there is always a logistics challenge around the corner. Patagonia is an astonishingly beautiful place, a natural wonder, and a thrill to visit, but it makes you work for your adventure - as we shall see.

They set off first to Torres del Paine with some borrowed hiking and camping gear from Rodrigo hiking the trails instead of running as they had to transport their own gear and set camp each night. Torres del Paine National Park has become an icon in the world of hiking and rock climbing. The park incorporates a spur of mountains that, although technically part of the Southern Andes range, are quite distinct in geological terms. A volcanic intrusion punched through the earth's crust 12 million years ago, lifting sedimentary rock to the sky atop the new igneous rock. The erosive powers of the weather over the millenia combined with many comings and goings of ice ages have left dramatic cathedrals of rocks, striped and coloured, jagged and sharp. The mountains are bounded on the west side by the southernmost extent of the Patagonian Ice Field, and are prominent from the surrounding low lying landscape to the south and east. The Patagonian Ice Field stretches for hundreds of miles and terminates at its southern tip with several glaciers - Grey, Tyndall, Gykkie and Pingo. The interface of these glaciers, the jagged formations of the mountain massif, several glacial lakes connected by rivers and waterfalls, and a surrounding landscape of tundra and forest make a truly amazing natural tapestry. The park derives its name from the centrepiece attraction of the mountain massif - three staggering towers of granite rising improbably to the sky. In the Aonikenk language of the indigenous Tehuelche people their word for blue was something sounding like *pie-nay* which in Spanish became Paine. The blue towers. Another word of Aonikenk was *pay-oh-way*, meaning hidden, that became Pehoe in Spanish, a name of one of the several beautiful glacial lakes below the massif. But many more natural features of the landscape have long since lost their native names. Instead they bear either Spanish names, Los Cuernos (the horns, another set of spiky rock formations) or are named after successive European explorers, Lago Nordenskjöld (after a Swedish explorer) or Tyndall Glacier (after an Irish glaciologist).

Those explorers, and those of today clad in rather less tweed, came in large part in the footsteps of one British woman - Lady Florence Dixie. She is credited as being one of the first outsiders to visit the area in 1878-88. 'Discovering places' was rather *en vogue* in Victorian high society in those days. Florence set out to challenge the contemporary view of a woman at the time, especially a woman married with children, and distinguished herself in an already adventurous family - her elder brother died descending from the first ever ascent of the Matterhorn in 1865. Her writings about her adventures inspire people to this day. Many still flock to explore the region as she did - by horseback. Many more visitors though now come to attempt one of the very popular hiking trails - the 'W' and the 'O' named due to their shape viewed on a map - or to attempt some of the world class rock climbing on the granite towers. Further adventure sports can be had at Glacier Grey where you can strap on a pair of crampons and hike out onto the glacier itself to view the stomach churning crevasses and statuesque ice formations up close. Kayaking amongst the icebergs on Lago Grey into which the glacier disgorged is also available. With so much on offer in the National Park and the surrounding region, the real challenge is finding the time to fit it all in, and finding favour with the weather gods to even attempt it.

Allison and Gabe did not have to wait long before they experienced firsthand the power of the weather. Allison got blown clean off her feet on one trail at a point aptly named - Paso del Viento, Windy Pass. Back on two feet, they bowed into the wind and trudged the rest of the hike up to the most famous view of the Torres del Paine massif - the base of the famous towers themselves. As Allison remembers it, "it felt like they were pretty." The towers were completely obscured behind fog and clouds - as they quite frequently are. Having hiked several hours to reach the viewpoint many visitors get this version of the towers - battered by swirling rain and howling wind, which defies all Goretex and soaks to the bone, they forlornly take their camera out and take a picture of the grim and grey reality before retreating down the mountain again. They also experienced firsthand the underwhelming food in the refugios and they got a feel for the pinch points of the park - where the concentration of visiting tourists was highest, and where the crowds could be avoided and peace and quiet found. "Raw, rugged, wild," are the three words Gabe offered as his first impression of the Paine massif. This was a place of elemental nature, where one accepts the buffeting by the wind, in order to enjoy the privilege of seeing the amazing landscape. They also visited Tierra del Fuego, the Land of Fire, as the first European visitors named it on seeing the many fires the indigenous inhabitants had lit along the coastline. Getting there involved "that crazy ferry ride where we thought the ferry would tip over," as Allison recalls it. On getting there one can visit penguin colonies, see vast prairies of sheep grazing alongside wild guanacos (a sort of llama cousin) and feel very small indeed in a huge landscape.

A typical view - or lack thereof - at the base of the Towers

The challenge for Allison, Gabe, Rodrigo and Nicolas, was to stitch these experiences together into a cohesive itinerary in a place where distances are large and transport is at the mercy of the weather. Most visitors come to Southern Patagonia with a lot of time - one could pass a few months and still miss a lot of sights and experiences. The beta version of Run Patagonia was an effort to put a few core Patagonian experiences alongside some epic runs. They would start by sailing the Strait of Magellan, whale watching and spotting seabirds as they went, to visit the far south of Tierra del Fuego and view some very remote and very epic glaciers. From there they would travel back across the big island of Tierra del Fuego itself, running en route, and then head northwest to reach Puerto Natales - base camp town for visiting Torres del Paine. They selected some runs inside and outside of the national park, and hikes where gear had to be carried, and incorporated a visit to a working sheep ranch, as well as opportunities for kayaking and ice trekking. They planned their own cook team to provide food they wanted when they wanted it. All this in ten days. The logistical challenges were many. Ambition was evident.

***

"A lot of the problems were weather related."

ALLISON

March 2015

After a year of many planning emails and much energy burned over the effort it took to get wire transfers into a Chilean bank account, the first logistical hurdle of Run Patagonia was finding a luggage cart in Mexico City. Allison and Gabe were flying all the way to the bottom of the Americas via Mexico City and Santiago. Along with their luggage they had a 14 feet by 16 feet canvas walled tent that had been custom made in Denver - the cook tent. Packed and compressed for transport it was a two person lift. Their wallets full of US Dollars and Chilean Pesos in anticipation of the expenses ahead, they lacked the 10 peso Mexican coin that would unlock a luggage cart and lift their burden. They checked in their dignity and begged. Supported by good Mexican charity they made it finally to Punta Arenas with all luggage intact and began the nervy process of awaiting the arrival of all the runners. Nervy because they had hired the aforementioned private boat to set off immediately from Punta Arenas and there could not be any waiting for latecomers. "A terrible idea," admits Allison now with years of experience of building buffers and wiggle room into itineraries. The gods of weather and flight connections initially were in their favour and everyone avoided ice storms in Texas to make it down to the tip of South America and on to the good ship Forrest on time.

Spirits were high on-board, fuelled by an open bar, and all the runners got to park their running shoes and get straight into the more important business of getting to know one another. The Forrest boat provided a remarkable setting to do so. Get-to-know-you conversations were frequently interrupted by humpback whale sightings. The boat would slow down and everyone would excitedly pour out of the cabin onto the deck to hear the enormous whales blow a couple of deep breaths, spraying water several feet in the air, before flicking their giant tailfins up as a goodbye salute and returning to the depths. Giant wandering albatrosses, petrels and gulls swooped and cut across the waves around the boat. Dolphins occasionally flashed past in busy leaping pods. It was an immersive way to plunge people from their long plane journeys and their lives at home into the wild marine world of the Strait of Magellan.

They got their first runs of the trip on the remote and lonely roads of Tierra del Fuego and everyone settled into the rhythm of the trip. They started to feel the pulse of a wild and untamed landscape - from the blustery wind to the tangy smell of the sea, from the ever changing skyscapes to the expanse of land all around which seemed almost forebodingly vast and empty. The guide team began to understand Chilean dinner time - a minimum of one hour later than advertised - and started adjusting communication to the runners accordingly. There is no worse feeling than anxious runners huddled around a table of empty plates unable to formulate conversation for want of calories. They also got used to answering the age old question of 'what will the weather be?' In Patagonia this is best answered with a hopeful smile and an admonition to always bring your raincoat. 'Fresh breeze' entered the daily forecast from the guide team - this covered all wind speeds up to 'can no longer run in a straight line'. Running in the far tip of South America there is simply no way to avoid getting battered like a sail - best to just enjoy the red cheeked wildness and blow snot rockets to your heart's content.

Several days of spectacular but windy running into the trip the group made it to the Torres del Paine section of the itinerary. At the Paine Grande *refugio* - named after the mountain peak under which it hunkers, the highest in the park - the group was retiring early for the night. The daily miles in the Patagonian wind had worn everyone out. Allison and Gabe were themselves worn out but seized on the downtime after everyone went to bed to relax together in the refugio common room and play a game of checkers. It had been all-go for the runners so far, and all-go for them also. The tent they had lugged to the bottom of the Americas was often the centre of action - early morning breakfast preparations and late evenings washing dishes. Lots of huddles with Rodrigo and Nicolas to try and stay a step ahead of the weather and logistics in a trip where every hour was planned for. Before they could fully switch off guiding mode though one of the runners popped into the common room with an announcement bearing eerie similarity to the one in a Nairobi hotel before the shattered door incident. "Uh, Gabe, could you come and take a look at this - there's an issue." Gabe only got to witness the aftermath of said issue, but based on testimony from the runners present we can picture the following scene.

Six of the runners were getting ready for bed in their dormitory - all the refugios in the national park have dorms with bunk beds. They were in good spirits, telling lots of jokes. One of the guys thought a particular joke was funny. Very funny. So very funny in fact, that he began to choke, and was struggling to breathe due to the convulsions of laughter. The others looked on with expressions gradually turning from amusement to concern. The choking laughter reached a crescendo whereby the contents of this gentleman's stomach disgorged - his chicken dinner was no more. As the vomit came forth he turned his head in a 180 degree arc and, improbably, managed to splatter 4 out of the 6 beds in the room with laughter vomit - "like a lawn sprinkler," Gabe suggests on reflection. Needless to say his bunkmates were less than enthused with him, and he was mortified, and no-one wanted to go to bed anymore. Gabe joined in viewing the massacre and then with resignation he traipsed off to the front desk. He tried bribery, flattery and begging on the staff who were less than interested and all felt it lay rather outside their scope of work. Eventually, and with an absolute absence of urgency, clean blankets were found and a makeshift arrangement made for the runners to bunk down in a spare room that had been conjured up in the packed refugio. An early night and relaxation time were both now out of the question as Gabe finally returned to the staff sleeping quarters after midnight. Unfortunately his ordeal was not over. What followed in that room was, as he describes it, "a snoring contest between Allison and the cook." He tossed and turned as logs were sawed all around him before he finally had an idea. At 2am in the morning he dragged his bedding down the hall and into the vomit dormitory. Window wide open he selected a non-splattered berth and slept, "like a little baby angel bear."

The next day the group headed off onto the trails of Torres del Paine again - chicken salad sandwiches in their lunch packs that no-one could eat after hearing of the previous night's antics - and into the teeth of an ever strengthening gale which bore down on them with a special kind of sideways rain that defies all rain jackets. The wind in this particular area of the park on the approach to Refugio Grey is ferocious. It storms off the ice field a few miles in the distance, funnels down between the mountains, a chilly bite added to it as it passes over the icy expanse of Grey Glacier, and it meets you full force - there is no shelter to be had. If they thought the weather had been stormy before this point it was about to get a lot worse over the coming days for the runners. Some of them had a bit of a struggle-fest on the way to reaching Refugio Grey where, it turned out, there could be no ice-trekking on the glacier or kayaking on the lake amongst the icebergs due to the powerful wind. Everyone hunkered down inside the *refugio*, rather relieved to not be outside anymore, and availed themselves of the well stocked bar. Whilst everyone mingled with other groups and hikers and guides also staying in the *refugio*, Allison and Gabe were put in a state of worry for the evening by an off-hand comment by one guide. "I hope the boat comes tomorrow," he stated casually, referring to the boat that they planned to take in the morning from the *refugio* down Lago Grey and to their waiting transport at the nearest road. A rather sinking feeling set in as they watch the tired but happy runners enjoy a well-earned beer and nurse their blisters and leg aches. What a nice surprise that would be for everyone to wake up if they had to turn around and go back out on the trail again on what was scheduled to be their rest day. Mercifully, next morning, the boat struggled through the wind and waves and the runners rejoiced.

They even got an up-close viewing of the glacier on their way out of the park to civilization. The glacier face, a hundred feet high or so, loomed over the passenger ferry and stretched for several miles across. Far more of its bulk unseen below the murky grey waters of the lake. A great place to feel small and wonder at the colossal forces of nature that have shaped our world.

Hopefully awaiting the boat that may or may not show up in Patagonia

The weather held them in its grip for the remainder of the trip. Rain caused rivers to surge and made the trail to the 'Base of the Towers' viewpoint inaccessible so they had to run elsewhere to round off the trip. It was a happy change though - they ran on other trails that offered phenomenal views of the Paine massif and its surrounding lakes. Even if it was Plan B, there are no bad plans in Torres del Paine and no ugly trails hiding away unused. Even when harried by the weather the rugged and wild landscape impresses.

All in all, once you've been exposed to the elements in Patagonia for several days you are happy with what you can get. You take the views you get and forget the ones you didn't. You embrace the elements and submit to the will of the weather gods.

As the runners headed back to the airport to migrate north again, the guide team regrouped and regathered and got ready for the second round. After just a couple of days break, they were awaiting another group of 16 runners to do it all again! Between trips they debriefed, making tweaks and alterations to the plan, and adding contingencies. The mantra for Patagonia has since become; Plan B isn't enough. You need Plan C, D and E as well. All in all though they felt the trip had been a tremendous success, they received great feedback as runners departed, and they were feeling good that trip number two would go even smoother now the groundwork had been laid. That eternal hope even crossed their mind - maybe the weather will be better.

None of Plans A through E involved getting stuck in an ice pack like Ernest Shackleton on his fateful Endurance expedition a century prior. But a day into the second trip, with a freshly arrived group of 16 runners, that was exactly the scenario they now faced. They had done this excursion with the previous group with no issues. After a night of motoring on board the Forrest boat to reach the fjords on the northern side of Alberto de Agostini National Park, everyone jumped into the more nimble zodiac boats in order to cruise up a fjord to view a glacier close-up and even make a landing in this most remote and inaccessible of places. It was during this landing process that things went rather awry. One by one, as the captain feathered the throttle, runners were hopping off the zodiac onto a large rock platform with a good view of the glacier face. A rather ominous crack boomed around the fjord. Initially no-one could see any ice actually calving off the glacier but then waves started to slam into the zodiac and the captain backed away from the rocks to ride over the swell. Gabe was among those already on the rock platform and they were now scooting around dodging waves that were sloshing chunks of ice at them. As the waves got a little more manageable the zodiac made its advances to approach the rock again and, with careful timing, one at time someone could jump off the rock again and into the zodiac. It was a lengthy process, though, as the waves continued to make it all rather precarious. All the while, wave after wave brought more and more ice out the fjord and it began to crowd around the craft. The second zodiac was at this point further away from the rock keeping watch in case the situation got worse but itself in no danger. Finally they were fully loaded again and turned away from the rocks and made their way out the fjord. Or at least they tried. It dawned on everyone bit by bit, that even with the engine fully throttled they were not going anywhere. They poked and prodded at the ice jam that had formed around them. The crew swung oars and even hung off the front to push with their feet. But it was all forlorn. They were stuck fast. Already wearied after a couple of weeks of dealing with Patagonia's curve balls, Allison and Gabe exchanged that 'what the actual fuck' look between them. Only courtesy had put them together on the same boat. Waiting out of etiquette until all the runners were loaded on to the boats before themselves taking the last two spots on the same craft. "At no point was anyone in any danger," Gabe is quick to point out to me at this point. The runners were just a bit bemused by it all. They were probably equally bemused when the Forrest boat turned up a short while later, cutting powerfully through the ice, and the crew of the large craft were out on deck with big smiles and their phones out taking pictures and videos of the stranded runners. It seemed that all of them, visitors and locals, were going to be using this as a good dinner party story for some time to come.

Temporarily "Shackleton-ed" off the south coast of Chile

"To this day, I've never been so stressed out," remembers Allison about this day and yet she wasn't referring to the fun and games in the ice jam at all. That was quickly laughed off as everyone got back on board the Forrest boat and they motored on to their final destination at a remote inlet. They disembarked and started their scheduled run for the day - an hour or two late due to the setbacks in the ice but nonetheless Allison remembers the run as, "one of the best 8 milers of my life." A remote stretch of dirt road, that often saw not a single car in a day, brought them gradually uphill to reach the beautiful and vast Lago Fagnano. When the running is good in the far south, it is really good. Glow in your cheeks as you get nipped by the chilly wind, vast serene wilderness all around, and the only sound is the crunch of your shoes on the dirt. Epic running. Gabe at the back of the group 'running sweep' was not feeling the running flow so much. He was tending to one of the runners as she soldiered through the run in a state of some distress. First diagnosis of lingering seasickness turned out to be wrong. It was, in fact, that worst friend of travellers everywhere - diarrhea. Without getting too lavatorial the run was a challenge, but everyone rallied around to help her to the finish. On completion of the run they synced up with Nicolas and their bus driver. Whilst they had been motoring down the Strait of Magellan, Nicolas had made the twelve hour drive across Tierra del Fuego, including a ferry from the mainland, to rendezvous with them here so they could drive to their rented farmhouse that was their accommodation for the night after the run. In a land of zero phone signal he was glad to finally see them rather later than he had expected. Nicolas took the sick runner and Allison with him in his pick-up to make best possible speed to the farmhouse whilst the rest of the group rode behind in the minibus. As night began to fall the remote road began to feel ever more remote, and the illness on board was not getting any better. The drive was punctuated with regular roadside pit stops as they wound their way up the dirt road switchbacks of a mountain pass. The headlight glare of Nicolas's pick-up was then filled with falling snow. First a few flurries and then steady driving snow fast becoming a white-out and slowing their progress to a crawl. Allison's stress levels were spiking. Her thoughts alternated between total helplessness and pity for her patient in the front seat, and visions of a busload of runners careering off the gravel road into the abyss somewhere behind them. There may even have been a few doubts about her life choices during that drive. What felt like an eternity was probably a couple of hours at most. Eventually, they made it to their rustic farmhouse in the middle of nowhere that had very basic amenities but at that moment looked like the Ritz Carlton. Rodrigo was waiting with a big pot of soup on the stove, a crackling blaze in the fireplace, a mound of blankets for their patient to dive under for an early night and everyone else could reflect on a day of rather more adventure than they had bargained for. They might have landed in Punta Arenas as strangers just over 24 hours previously, but they were all very much bonded by now.

Little did they know how much more bonded they were to become. The following morning their patient had bounced back and even joined the group again for an early morning run across the snow covered, serene emptiness around the farmhouse. The bug that had ailed her had probably already achieved its sole purpose - to spread. Over the next 48 hours Gabe plus about half of the group succumbed to the carnage and the roadsides of Tierra del Fuego bore the brunt. By the time they arrived at Puerto Natales a little over a day later Allison had become the bug angel - herself impervious to all known travel illness then and since - and was placing bottles of Sprite and packets of plain crackers outside hotel room doors. She headed off with the healthy half of the group to a planned farm tour and dinner outside of town. Despite skittishness around the group every time someone so much as moved to go for a pee, they were over the hump and the bug was no more. They were now truly bonded by their war stories and, restored to full health, ready to tackle Torres del Paine. It could only get better, right?

For the first group Grey Glacier had been a hostile inaccessible menace on the horizon as they struggled up to the refugio near the glacier's calving front. In hostile conditions with wind screeching and visibility reduced to a few feet it is hard to imagine why anyone would want to go near the glacier, let alone go on top of it. For the second group it was a different world. The runners strapped crampons on to their Hokas and Nikes and walked out onto a benign surreal ice world - the weather was splendid. To see people's faces must be a joy for the ice trekking guides who do the excursion every day all season - adults overcome with the wide eyed and slack-jawed wonder of little kids. As you crunch around on top of the glacier you get a sense of the vastness. The glacier stretches off miles and miles into the distance, contorted and folded, flowing as a river of ice from the plateau of the ice field above, down between the mountains to the lake. It is one of those places to absorb, channel your sense of wonder, appreciate what a fortunate little moment it is to be alive and in that precise geographic location at that precise moment of earthly history. If you've had explosive diarrhea for a couple of days of your trip you might feel you've bloody earned it as well.

All of the runners bar one savoured the experience of trekking on the glacier. One of the runners, Keri, joined Allison for kayaking instead as her ankle was causing bother and crampons and ice didn't seem to be a wise combination. Keri had sprained her ankle earlier in the trip and, in classic runners' fashion, was basically ignoring it and continuing to run and hike on it as best she could. She skipped the ice trekking in order to give herself the best shot at the grand finale of the trip - the trail up to the 'Base of the Towers' viewpoint. The rivers had receded, the trail was open, and the weather was, improbably, quite balmy. Harmless puffy white clouds floated across the blue sky as Keri mummified her ankle with strapping, acquired a set of hiking poles, and even hired a gaucho to give her a ride part way up the trail on his horse. She was pulling out all the stops and was not going to give in. With the help of the group, steely determination saw her to the viewpoint which rewarded her with the picture perfect view. Vast granite spikes stretching to the blue sky, a fringe of snow and ice cloaking their base like a scarf, and an aquamarine blue lake in the foreground. Ankle swelling is forgotten for such a view. The group celebrated as a whole - bonded by their trials and tribulations of the past days and buoyed by the perfect finale.

Well-deserved sunny skies in Patagonia

Such was the arc of the story the group had been on that Allison and Gabe were struck by an idea that was to be a keeper. They decided that each person in the group would receive a personalised award of sorts. A little memento to their part of the story. On the last night of the trip the dinner concluded with an informal ceremony. Keri of course was commemorated for the bravery and stubbornness of soldiering on through injury - a stress fracture was later confirmed back in Austin - and others were called out for less lofty achievements. 'Top bunk' was the name of one award for someone who had indulged with rather too much good Chilean wine on the Forrest boat and rolled out of the top bunk - repeatedly - during the first night of the trip. Slamming into the floor of the boat to the startlement of their bunkmates - a cracked rib the penalty for that overindulgence. This final night award ceremony with the group has become a fixture on all the international trips ever since. A chance to laugh and remember, part roast and part tribute, a chance to build some runners up, or to knock some down! Every group in every place takes on its own unique story due to the personalities of the runners and the unpredictable things that arise in the course of travel. In Patagonia runners receive as an award the simple token of a jar of locally made Calafate berry jam. No medals - just a representation and a memento. The Calafate is especially fitting due to the local legend that says, 'if you eat the Calafate berry you will always come back to Patagonia.'

Patagonia is that kind of a place. When you leave, you want to go back. In your mind's eye you can still feel the wind. You can remember the cold and the rain. Yet the raw beauty and power of the place calls like a siren. The privilege of experiencing one of the world's true wild places is alluring. Even if there will be bumpy roads to travel, bad weather to endure, and plans continually changing from A to B to let's just see. The challenge of the place and the weather makes one more grateful for the good moments, when the morning light hits the granite towers of Torres del Paine a certain way, or you catch a sunset by the Rio Serrano as the salmon leap and the *gauchos* round up the horses for the day. Those little moments become even more cherished.

In the years since those first trips the itinerary has changed, the local partners have changed, the food has changed for the better - the only thing that has stayed the same is the weather. It is still changeable. It is a trip of continual evolution. Tweaking and modifying in reaction to each different tourism season in the far south. The cook tent has been jettisoned as better options emerged on the culinary front. The Forrest boat is no longer in service. Patagonia continues to pitch curve balls and force ever more savvy trip planning methods. But we love it so. Let it never get easy - it is supposed to be an adventure. Perhaps Ernest Shackleton himself put it best when he said, "difficulties are just things to overcome, after all."

| 7 |

Off the Map: Slovenia

The average American adult, tasked with filling in the names of countries on a blank outline map of Europe, would probably get through the bigger, Western countries fairly easily. Italy looks like a leg with a boot. Easy. France is way over there right next to Britain. On a roll. Spain is down below that. Making progress now. Those cold Nordic places are up top somewhere, not totally sure which one is which, but they're all the same, right? Then as attention slides towards central Europe and moves ever further east thoughts get a little hazy. Convictions begin to falter. There are all those countries that end in 'ia'. Is Czechoslovakia still a thing? No they split up, ok, right. Yugoslavia also split up into a whole bunch of countries, right? Oh Greece! I know Greece, it is over here somewhere in the east part of the Mediterranean. All the islands - I heard Santorini is a-ma-zing. Ask them to drop a pin on Slovenia though, and you've got yourself a great game of pin the tail on the donkey. To be fair to our imaginary American geography scholar, many less travelled Europeans might struggle to pin the location of Slovenia as well. It is there, hiding in plain sight. Boasting the eastern edge of the Alps, a section of beautiful Adriatic Sea coastline, stunning wine country, enchanting castles, and beautiful traditional towns and cities. At the time of writing the singular tourist attraction of Lake Bled, with its postcard perfect church on an island view, has propelled Slovenia into more widespread tourist consciousness. Back in April 2015, shortly after the first Patagonia trips, when a cold email hit the Rogue Expeditions inbox it is fair to say that even Lake Bled wasn't much on the radar.

The email came from Borut and his friend Tone - two Slovenian guys that met during their studies in Austin at the University of Texas and forged a friendship over shared pride in their homeland and a love of water polo. They had been hitting ideas back and forth between themselves about a small tourism venture that would bring Americans to Slovenia and let them discover the best sights and the culinary delights. They both had their 'real jobs' so this would be a side gig, a passion project, an exploration to see what was possible and to keep them connected to home. Borut came across the newly emerging notion of a 'runcation' and thought that would be just the ticket for Slovenia. He was a keen runner and knew many of boundless possibilities for trails that could be explored in his homeland. The power of the Austin running community intervened and someone suggested to him he should check out Rogue Expeditions. A quick rummage on Google and he landed on roguexpeditions.com (Allison and Gabe do know how to spell and are quite aware there is an 'e' seemingly missing in their URL. However rogueexpeditions.com was taken by some big game hunters in Alaska. This crucial 'e' defines whether you want to shoot the animals you find when out exploring in nature with an iPhone or a rifle). He liked what he saw on their site and fired off an email making an introduction.

On receipt of that email Allison flagged it and put it away as a possibility to think about. There is always the chance that such an email passes through one's inbox unconsidered. At the time there were a lot of runners cold emailing Rogue to offer their services as a run guide in exchange for some 'free' travel. Those got filed away unflagged. This email seemed a little different though and piqued her interest - especially as Borut was in Austin and available to meet in person. She then rummaged on Google for a place called Slovenia. She says now that she, "may have heard of Slovenia," before that email from Borut. She hovers on the word 'may' here. Gabe is less tentative and claims he knew of the country, "but didn't know a whole lot about it." At that time Gabe was heading to the Grand Canyon again for a couple of weeks on a river rafting trip. He was ready for dropping off grid and resuming his morning routine of sitting on his groover by the side of the Colorado River enjoying the morning light glowing on the canyon walls. No cell service. No technology. Just paddling all day with good friends and camping on sandy river banks under the stars each night - not even a tent needed in the dry climate. Upon his return to the world he headed back to Austin where the RV was parked for the winter and they were back living in their house temporarily. A new concept called Airbnb was making its emergence around this time and allowing them to rent out their house on a short term basis that suited their needs and gave a fixed base for the cooler, more enjoyable winter months in Austin.

Despite the extended pause due to the rafting trip, Borut got a response to his email and ABGB, one of the many excellent Austin craft breweries, was selected to host an exploratory meeting. Allison and Gabe had fairly low expectations about the meeting but figured it was polite to meet-up and it couldn't hurt to hear about a country they knew fairly little about. Borut, on the other hand, came prepared. With a round of beers they huddled around Borut's laptop on which he had a whole presentation prepared and many pictures to showcase the place they would see. Athletic, energetic, and confident, Borut is made for moments of salesmanship like this. With smooth delivery he quickly bypassed any objections they might have had about being able to sell a trip to a destination that was at the time quite niche. The trip would begin in Venice and end in Croatia he explained. Bookend the itinerary with known tourist destinations but make the meat of the trip full of lesser known gems in Slovenia. He reeled off knowledge of Michelin starred restaurants in this town or that one, farms with guest houses belonging to people he personally knew, specialty dishes and Slovenian wine and liqueurs, trails that he had run in the mountains of Triglav National Park or along the coastline of Croatia's Istrian peninsula. His worldly self-confidence is of the infectious type, giving you no room to doubt, and he steered them through the presentation answering questions before they could be posed. He showed pictures of the Soča river with its startling blue waters only to better them with shots of the inviting azure waters of the Adriatic Sea from the islands off Croatia. Besides the running there could be river rafting, private boat hires, wine making tours and visits to castles. It was pretty clear he hadn't come to the beer meeting for just a beer. Allison and Gabe went home and started immediately looking at plane tickets to Europe. Such was the back-to-back nature of their 2015 calendar; however, it would be several months before a scouting trip could actually happen.

* * *

"Our goal was to create special moments in already special places."

BORUT

November 2015

After guiding trips to Kenya and then Morocco, they arrived in Venice in November, rather at the end of the tourist season for Europe. Firstly, they dived into an Airbnb apartment in the heart of the city for a couple of days rest and recuperation. After guiding back to back to back trips there was laundry to address, emails stacking up, social media posts to be scheduled, trip photographs to edit and distribute, expenses to collate, and any cravings to attend to - good coffee and chocolate for Allison, chips and salsa for Gabe. The Texan reader will immediately know what I mean by chips and salsa, but I should specify that these are crispy, oven baked tortilla chips, ideally served warm, with a liberal portion of hot and spicy tomato salsa. Gabe has at the time of writing ordered chips and salsa off many menus in many countries to varying degrees of disappointment. One skeptical waitress in South Africa a few years back assured him that she knew what he meant and then furnished him with a large bowl of soggy french fries accompanied by a gloopy pool of marinara sauce. Allison tells me his face was just a picture. Clean laundry in hand and cravings satiated they set out from their Airbnb recovery camp and tentatively explored a damp and rainy Venice whilst getting attacked by hordes of umbrella-wielding tourists seemingly at every turn. Borut's notes and plan had seemingly foreseen this as he planned for the group to stay at a guesthouse on a private island away from downtown Venice itself. Borut recalls preparing the trip to be presented to Rogue. He tells me that he and Tone sought to include, "special moments in already special places," and this private island was just one such example. They sought the extra mile, the creative extra detail. In doing so they, "packed the schedule to the gills," on the first iteration. They felt they had a lot to show, and on their side were, "apprehensive and had doubts," that they could deliver a worthy experience. Feeling the positive kind of pressure of presenting their part of the world in a good light perhaps.

Borut himself wasn't in the country at the time but his friend, business partner, fellow Longhorn alumni, and former water polo teammate, Tone, met them and was to play host for the coming days. Tone is one of those people who can immediately put anyone he meets at ease. He has an ability to engage in meaningful conversation with someone he has just met. He cuts through any constipated introductory conversation and gets straight into the good stuff. Tall, broad shouldered, and powerfully built, he will admit he is no longer in his best water polo shape but he still cuts an imposing figure. As a host he is in his element. He whisked them away from the umbrellas of Venice and drove them a couple of hours to stay with his wife Petra in Ljubljana. Their hosts immediately and rapidly deployed delicious home cooked food, and uncorked excellent and underrated Slovenian wine, and Allison and Gabe were in no doubt from the start that this was someone they would be confident working with. On top of the good impression Borut had made there was the feeling of another great team in the making. Tone echoed this feeling when I asked about his first impressions, "immediately I got the positive energy."

By his own admission Tone isn't much of a runner but he happily drove Allison and Gabe around the countryside in the following days as they followed somewhat cryptic written directions from Borut on the best places to run. Tone dropped them off at trailheads at beautiful spots like Lake Bled, Lake Bohinj, Bovec and the Soča Valley and then waited patiently at the other end of the trails in the hope the American visitors would emerge some time the same day. Borut had supplied them with a lot of written bullet points that seemed to have been written from memory about forks in the trail, possible landmarks, probable key turns, nice viewpoints and so on. What he hadn't supplied was any GPS data or maps. These days, scouting runs has become a rather more technological affair with precise data from watches, terrain surveys from Google Earth and global ordnance survey maps, turns in the run preloaded into a navigation app on a smartphone or into the GPS watch itself, and of course phone data coverage virtually globally in case you need to pull up a map on the run. Somehow the innocent days, just a few years back, of a few vague bullet points of written description are more exciting. Disappearing off into the Slovenian mountains in hope rather than expectation. Furthermore, during these initial years for Rogue, the concept of a GPS wristwatch was changing dramatically. Bulky, cumbersome, devices that looked more suited for tracking annual migration whilst strapped to the back of a whale, got replaced by ever smaller and more accurate gadgets. Calculating running distances had once been done by measuring in a car! Or by roughly knowing your average typical running speed i.e. I ran for an hour so let's call that a 10 miler. Bit by bit runners were turning up on Rogue trips with these watches and correcting run distances. Hamid's Land Cruiser in Morocco might have told them a run through the Sahara on a rough, rocky patch of sand was 12 miles or so. Now runners would hit the finish line, tell them they only had 11.73 miles on their watches and then start running off the other direction again to make up the 0.27 miles - a process known as gerbiling after those small, furry, dedicated, four-legged, distance runners! In time, Strava and TrainingPeaks and other training plat-forms would take this data collection to a whole other level of ob-session. All of this was far from Borut's mind when he shared his cryptic trail notes. He admits here that to begin with he, "wasn't very good at it" and didn't quite know, "what might make a good run or a bad run."

Gabe somewhere on a Croatian mountainside, scouting a rocky route that did not make the cut

All that is to say that they got lost rather a lot. Many fences were climbed over, and then re-climbed over. Many trails dead-ended. Many times they simply ended up in a field with a few nonplussed cows. Regardless, the running was beautiful. It was storybook coun-tryside. They ran through green fields, past charming farmsteads and alpine style *chalets*, through pristine forests and around clear and tranquil lakes, scored big mountain views as well as quaint village scenes. It was a wonderful bucolic countryside, quintessentially European, matching rural alpine feel with ancient, storied, villages and towns. The quality of the running was matched by the cuisine at the end of each day. Borut's trail route descriptions might have lacked accuracy, but his restaurant and guesthouse recommendations were on point. Menus were rarely available, rather dishes chosen by the chef arrived unbidden and Tone curated the whole experience explaining origins of ingredients and dishes. Most places tended to have a special set menu for the day in keeping with seasonal produce and their particular style. With an emphasis on locally grown high quality produce Slovenian cuisine deftly borrows from Balkan tradition whilst integrating the best of Italian food and Central European fare as well. Hearty soups or stews, fine pastries and sweet desserts, platters of cheese and dried meats, and flavour packed slow cooked meats. At a typical ten course dinner (ten is a very reasonable number of courses in Slovenia) you might encounter risottos, pasta, goulash, schnitzel, dumplings, and a dozen different ways to fill a štruklji (a sort of roll pastry filled with...well, many different things!). All this was accompanied by excellent Slovenian wines and typically the finale was some mystery home brewed alcohol as a *digestif*. You don't have to worry about what you feel like eating in Slovenia, rather you take a seat and embrace the experience until the end.

Just as Slovenian cuisine incorporates various regional influences its entire sense of national identity straddles a sort of divide in Europe. Tone again curated this part of Slovenia's make-up with ease having the benefit of both insider and outsider perspective. During the breakup of Yugoslavia Slovenia was the first new republic to emerge and it quickly asserted itself on the European stage in its own right. In the thirty years since it has become an integral part of the European Union. Progressive and integrated with its western neighbours, adopting the Euro currency, and trending towards that lofty goal of the EU itself - an ever closer union. Yet it achieved this with no loss of its heritage and history. No loss of identity or its own national beliefs. As it moved forwards and outwards it maintained close ties and good relations to its Balkan neighbours to the east seeming to straddle an apparent divide with relative ease. It is a physical crossroads, a cultural bridge, it is both east and west at once. In Ljubljana for example, a visitor can glimpse remnants of Iron Curtain history but feel as much a part of a modern European city as Paris or Amsterdam. This ability to hold on to history and yet move forward, to maintain traditional culture whilst embracing new ones, is a lesson well worth seeing for visitors.

Copious amounts of local food & wine is a highlight of any trip to Slovenia

Food amply sampled, wine extensively surveyed, history lessons conveyed, many trails run in circles, and guesthouses visited, Borut and Tone had succeeded with their vision and Slovenia was added to the Rogue Expeditions calendar for the following Autumn of 2016. They called the trip Run Alpe-Adria. The title aimed to capture the variety that the itinerary incorporated. A regional trip rather than a single destination. Starting with the canals of Venice, they would then spend a couple of days in the Julian Alps of Slovenia's Triglav National Park, then head south through the heart of Slovenia seeing epic castles and vineyards en route to Croatia's Istrian peninsula. A visit to one of the idyllic Croatian islands would follow and then complete the circle by travelling back to Venice at the finish. 3 countries in 9 days, mountains, forests, beaches, the best of European city culture and rural scenes straight out of The Sound of Music. It was an easy sell to a now expectant community of Rogue Expeditions runners, some of whom awaited announcements of new trip destinations with passports already in hand. The group of people who had already been on a trip was growing steadily and this group came to be known as the Rogue alumni. This crew started turning up for second and third trips, and beyond. The alumni became an important force in pulling in new runners, bringing friends, recommending to colleagues, wearing Rogue Expeditions hats and t-shirts wherever they ran, and starting conversations with interested runners. They became the evangelicals of the runcation world.

* * *

September 2016

A year on from initial scouting a group of runners was about a week out from arriving in Venice to kick off the first trip. Borut was on ground with Allison and Gabe and the three of them had a busy week ahead dialing in the last minute details and finalising a few of the run routes that would involve rather less jumping over fences. Gabe recollects one of the first of these runs vividly for me, "it was memorable for all the wrong reasons." After a late night arrival into Ljubljana from the US, the alarm-clock sounded at 4am and they hit the road south to Croatia to catch the first ferry of the day to the island of Cres. Jetlagged and somewhat undernourished from a Euro on-the-go breakfast consisting of a small croissant and a coffee, they eventually reached the start point of the run around 9 a.m., just as the heat was building on the Croatian coastline. Despite bodies complaining after many hours of plane time and then car time, they figured they would just suck it up and get the run done. Borut procured a litre of water each for everyone but Gabe pulled the short straw and ended up with a bottle of carbonated water. Undeterred, Gabe ignored a few stomach grumbles, ignored the slosh of warm fizzy water in the hydration bladder of his running backpack, and started the futile mission of keeping up with Allison and Borut - for 19 miles of exposed island terrain. Not a cloud in the sky to hide under, he ground out the miles through the shimmering landscape after the two dots of Borut and Allison always a few hundred yards distant. The hours passed, the heat increased, the sweat was profuse, the water in his pack was ever warmer and gassier, but finally they reached the quaint country farmhouse that marked the finish line of the run. Food and beverages were not forthcoming though. Borut had a restaurant recommendation in mind for them to check out. Gabe was too tired to argue one way or the other. So they all bummed a ride back across the island, collected the car, waited an excruciating hour for a ferry back to mainland, and finally at about 8pm that evening collapsed in a fancy restaurant to eat something substantial for the first time in well over 24 hours. The sweaty, dishevelled runners, probably pawing at fancy dishes like cavemen, must have done nothing for the decorum that evening.

A little over a week later, the new route on Cres was a hit when they returned with the group of runners. The temperatures were cooler, the group were well acclimated a few days into the trip with decidedly better sleep and nutrition levels than Gabe had during the scouting run and, all told, there was much more running flow. The route passed through quiet village streets and along old winding roads and rocky trails though a sage-scented landscape that seemed stuck in history. Red-roofed villages came and went between forested hills and sleepy farms with sheep outnumbering humans - all the while the Adriatic Sea gleamed on the horizon and offered refreshing sea breezes. Magic running. The reward for the group finishing the longest run of the trip was a privately chartered boat for a cruise along the Adriatic until sunset. Endorphins were flowing after the big run was done, good vibes were setting in as the whole group gorged on grilled fish and a buffet of other goodies on board the boat. The crew on board the boat topped up wine glasses before they ever got empty (a common quirk of Slovenian hospitality, not without consequence, which has led to many other stories that must be consigned to the cutting room floor rather than remembered in this book). Chilled sunset music turned into disco and, although you might think 19 miles might have knocked the stuffing out of the intrepid runners, they were running the 20th mile by hitting the makeshift dance floor on the aft deck of the boat. The scene was pretty magical - sunset hues began to stretch over the western horizon, the blue waters turning into reds and oranges, and the boat cruised along over gentle swell. The group cheered each other on as the dancing got a little more progressive, or as Gabe remembers it, "people were getting pretty loose."

The good wine was by now all finished and homebrew liquor was being drained out of mysterious unmarked jugs. Loose indeed. The post-run endorphins continued to surge. Gabe was unwinding too, soaking in the good energy of a great day and enjoying the high spirits all around. Just as he was indulging this moment a lady familiar to us was about to burst the bubble. Yvette - yes, same one again - of earlier note for missing a flight from Madrid to Marrakech (wine related), and shattering a glass shower door in Nairobi (mud related), was happily dancing above the deck on a bench at the side of the boat when she tottered overboard into the Adriatic sunset, smoothly clearing the safety railing en route (wine related). Before Gabe could get a 'holy shit' out of his mouth Tone dived overboard after her, thinking nothing of the 15ft drop to the waves below, his deeply ingrained water polo skills rushing to the fore. Most of the dancers were oblivious. They were lost in their hard earned reverie. Thankfully not everyone was hitting the homebrew though. The captain was alerted and he popped a prompt U-turn to go and scoop up Tone and Yvette from their sunset swim - thankfully she was none the worse for wear. A somewhat abashed group kicked the music from disco back to chill, dancing became subdued and self-conscious again, a soggy Yvette sat on the bench rather than dance on top of it, and the homebrew liquor jugs were banished to the galley.

Enjoying an afternoon on the Adriatic - pre-dance party

The high point of the trip in terms of running was arguably to be found in the heart of Triglav National Park by the Soča River. Starting near the river's source, in a beautiful valley under the shadow of some of Slovenia's highest peaks which rise thousands of feet above the valley floor, the Soča River Trail meanders with the river through pristine forests crisscrossing the river several times on picturesque footbridges. The Soča is everything a river should be - lively and turbulent, with waterfalls and canyons, shallows and torrents, rich in colour and character. The river really is a startling blue. Like you haven't seen this kind of blue before. In Autumn especially, the river's blue is framed by a thousand shades of russets, oranges, and rusty browns in the surrounding forest bringing theatre to the valley. Up high above the peaks are already dusted with snow but mostly hidden by low, damp, lazy clouds. The first Rogue group in Slovenia, encountering the trail at its Autumn best, also got to experience the forest trails at their pungent best. Never has decay smelt so good as the forest floors along the Soča. With leaves beginning their annual breakdown, and with Beech nuts coating the ground like mischievous marbles, the damp forest is heavy with a rich earthy scent. To run in such a forest is to experience what used to be. So many Alpine valleys are irrevocably altered by man, with farming, skiing, and logging etched into the landscape. The Soča has in recent decades been allowed to return to the wild and find its primeval self - its full expression.

Allison recounts for me that at least one out of the first Rogue group seemed to be connecting deeply with the surroundings during the run. Perhaps finding her true self. Everyone in the group had sucked in the air, exhaled a few wows on the suspension bridges over the river, and had a few mindful moments as they ran the miles down the valley towards the town of Bovec. Allison was 'the sweep' for the run accompanying the back of the pack, and they reached Tone a couple of miles from the finish of the run. Tone was manning a pop-up aid station offering snacks, river chilled beers, and directions towards the finish line of the run. Across the river from Tone sitting on a rock seemingly watching the flow go by was Martha. Allison waved. Martha waved back. The roar of the river was too loud for any verbal communication. "I think Martha is meditating," explained Tone with an understanding nod, "maybe she wants some alone time." Allison accepted this somewhat quizzically and chatted with the last runners for a few moments. "You're almost finished," said Tone to the last runners, "just continue right across the river." They left Allison with Tone and jogged off following the trail along the river towards the final bridge that would cross the river one more time and reach the run finish and lunch spot. Allison mulled for a moment on the precise wording Tone had used. She glanced across at Martha again. The penny dropped. This time Martha's wave looked less like 'hello' and more like 'where the fuck is the trail?' Allison waved back at her, windmilling Martha to come back across to this side. Martha gesticulated back again - her waving tone now suggesting that the water was pretty goddamn cold and running pretty goddamn fast and she didn't fancy another crossing. Tone seemed satisfied she was still meditating. Allison windmilled again, beckoning her across with more urgency. Finally a final wave from Martha indicated - 'fuck it, I'm going, I'm going.' She struggled through the waist deep water fighting to keep balance against the flow and emerged in a dripping puddle beside Allison and Tone.

"He said right across the river," Martha explained with a shrug, "I figured all the others just chickened out." Communication break-down resolved with laughs all around, her and Allison set off all smiles for the last stretch of running. The key detail in this episode was that Martha was a dedicated trail runner rather than the major-ity of the runners who had come on trips to date who were mainly roadies. To a trail runner it seems perfectly reasonable that the way forward could be wading 100ft across freezing, waist-deep, fast flowing water. Or straight up the mountain. Or straight through a bog. Trail runners see the natural world with different eyes in this way. There is always a way forward. Runners like Martha were a sign of things to come for Rogue, as more and more trail runners started to sign up for trips. In tandem with this, and with the run-ning in Slovenia and Croatia featuring prime examples, the trips themselves began to involve more and more trail running. Often the feeling for the guide team was one of bringing road runners from the city into the wild. Setting them free for the first time onto rutted and rocky trails through forests and mountains. Mostly this experience was highly fulfilling and rewarding. Occasionally it pro-vided some guiding challenges.

Two runners enjoy a mid-run refreshment; Martha is somewhere behind them, on the other side of the river

On a subsequent Slovenia trip, the run at Lake Bohinj, a beautiful alpine lake surrounded by forest cloaked mountains, started off very technical. In a torrential Autumn downpour, tree roots, sloppy mud, and treacherous chunks of limestone, were combining to make the trail more of a slip-n-slide than a runnable path. Jacob Garcia, better known as Jgar, a speedy Austinite more comfortable hammering out six minute miles on the road, navigated the morass nimbly emerging after a couple of miles on to a nice flat grassy meadow right by the lake itself. He promptly fell flat on his face. More accurately his arm got in the way of falling on his face. The arm broke his fall, and then the fall broke his shoulder. Unperturbed by this he decided to run a little faster to catch up with Allison who was out in front of the pack marking the route as she ran. Allison was already dealing with another issue - the trail had been closed due to previously unadvertised logging work in the area. In pouring rain and with body temperature plummeting, she attempted to pan the map on her soggy smartphone with numb fingers. Jgar zoomed up to her and asked 'how it was going' and she started to explain they were going to backtrack a little to a different trail. "Oh ok," said Jgar agreeably, "I think maybe I dislocated my shoulder," he decided to add. There followed an afternoon best categorised under 'guiding challenges.' Allison and Jgar struggled in the rain to pop his shoulder back into socket but to no avail. He had dislocated it several times before so wasn't too alarmed and in the end the only option was to run a couple more miles to reach Tone and a ride to a nearby medical clinic. Allison zipped around herding runners onto the rerouted trail whilst organising for an additional vehicle to come pick up the group so they could dispatch Jgar to medical help without delay. Hastily arranged pizza and coffee placated wet runners at the end of the run who were suffering due to the resulting delay.

Stories like this one capture the reality of the role of the run guide. On the face of it the role seemed straightforward. Prepare trip logistics. Liaise with local partners (after finding dependable ones like Borut and Tone). Lead runs. Provide information and interpretation for the clients. Ensure group security and safety. But there was also a large category of 'other duties as required'. These were the myriad things that could pop up. Unforeseeable occurrences that required fast thinking and fast action. Problem solving and improvisation. In the course of 2015 Allison and Gabe led 9 trips together in 5 locations. During 2016 the addition of Run Alpe Adria took them to 12 trips in 6 locations. They had by now a good understanding of what the role of a run guide involved. They were also fast approaching the point that exceeded what the two of them alone could manage. Thankfully more dominoes were always falling into the game - their burgeoning network would again provide.

| 8 |

Same Places, New Faces:
Morocco

"Don't worry, I will send this Irish guy Sean!"

JOSUE

In the early summer of 2015 Dacia, one of the runners from the second Run Morocco trip in 2014, was out there doing things that the Rogue Expeditions alumni were tending to do at this point. She was in a Seattle running store, evangelising about her runcation experience in Morocco and she dropped off some advertising flyers with the staff. One of those staff was Katie Conlon, who had moved from her native North Dakota to Seattle, and who worked part-time at the Trailhead running store for extra cash as well as being on the books with Brooks Running. Simply put Katie is more an Allison runner than a Gabe runner. She's fast, tall, elegant, and makes running look easy covering the ground with long smooth strides. She ran competitively in high school, continued to compete in college, and had high ambitions to build her life around competitive running for years to come. Intrigued by the Rogue flyer she sent off a hopeful introductory email along with her CV. Much like when Borut emailed, proximity was to play a role in getting a response. The Rogue RV was parked for the summer on a hay farm in Bend as Allison and Gabe were prepping for the upcoming trips there. An agreement was quickly reached to meet in Portland, roughly halfway between Seattle and Bend, where Allison and Gabe were planning to go anyway to set-up a promotional table at a running event hosted by the North Portland 'No-Po' running group. Such promo tables were part of the marketing ground game that was central to the Rogue sales strategy at the time - bring in just one new runner and you might seed a new customer base in a town like Portland with a big running community. No Facebook advertisement or search engine optimization can replace the impact of shaking hands with runners and telling them your story.

They all met up for a beer at a local Portland bar before the event. They were already impressed that Katie had driven 5 hours to something that wasn't even an official job interview. Allison's response to Katie's email had been along the lines of, 'we aren't hiring, and we don't have any money to do so, but you sound great, your running CV is solid, and we would love to meet you.' Katie makes a good first impression. Bright eyed and bushy tailed seems a fair description. She has a big ready smile, bright blue eyes and, imprinted by a South Dakota upbringing, the easy way of striking up a conversation that country people tend to have. She and Allison immediately had a lot in common in terms of being serious high school and college runners who were coming to focus on the marathon distance. They also had similarities in that they were entrenched in running communities and had a network of people to whom they could pitch Rogue trips. To begin with Katie represented a solid lead into the Seattle running community, a very able runner to help guide the runs on the Bend and Tahoe trips, a great bubbly personality to add to the guide team dynamic, and in time she became nothing less than part of the family. The domestic trips at Tahoe and Bend were relatively close to her and as they grew in the coming years her summer became centred around them. She and Gabe became the dream team for those trips. Washing dishes, cooking and cleaning, driving the vans to trailheads, running out front marking the trails, getting great pictures and videos of the clients, creating great energy and good vibes - whatever the task they threw themselves into it each summer as the domestic US getaways in many ways became the gateway drug to the wider Rogue world of running trips. Runners could try their first 'runcation' without leaving the US, with just a short domestic flight, and with the trips only lasting 5 days they could do it without blowing their vacation days for the year. During Tahoe or Bend they could meet Katie, Allison and Gabe and put faces to the brand and the company. Hear their stories about Morocco, Kenya, Patagonia and Slovenia - stories that were getting added to each year. Almost invariably if a runner had come on a domestic trip the next stop was international.

Katie Conlon (third from left) joined the team in 2016 and quickly became a key part of the US-based trips

Another conversation that started up around the same time as the email exchange with Katie was with Josue Stephens, a race director based in Austin at the time. Josue was traveling in Morocco in 2015 and noticed some posts from Morocco on the Rogue Running Facebook and Instagram channels. Intrigued, he reached out to Ruth, one of the owners of Rogue Running and Allison's boss, who informed him about the Rogue Expeditions concept. Josue's creative juices were flowing in Morocco. Inspired by the landscape, the toughness and ingenuity of the people - especially the mountain Berber peoples of the Atlas Mountains - Josue's brain started to do what it had pretty much always done: imagine a race. Josue in 2015 already had several years of directing ultra endurance races under his belt. He had fallen in love with long distance 100 km and 100 mile races a decade earlier and over time moved his passion from competing in them to organising them. He was involved in producing races throughout the US and Mexico and had created a race in Nicaragua that went on to gain folkloric status in the ultra-running community - the Fuego y Agua ultramarathons on the unique volcanic island of Ometepe. This event in particular gained a sort of legendary status, especially one of the races that Josue named Survival Run. This event saw runners tackle a course of unknown distance, a 24 hour time limit, with little or no course marking, encountering natural obstacles and challenges *en route* - harvesting and carrying bamboo, climbing coconut trees, hauling loads of plantains, no aid stations or medical support, and ferocious unforgiving terrain along the way, namely two rather large volcanoes. The race challenged competitors with the moniker - 'you will not finish.' It was a race about failure rather than success. Wearing competitors down to breaking point such that only 5% of starters reached the finish.

These thoughts were in Josue's mind as he admired the lifestyles and skills of the mountain Berbers of the High Atlas on his long trail runs through Morocco. There was enough common ground between Fuego y Agua and Rogue Expeditions to start up a dialogue and see what might be explored as a joint venture. The brands had a similar ethos and inspiration - to connect people to culture and places through the act of running. With Josue's creativity and connections to the endurance running world and Rogue's know-how and connections in Morocco and existing client base - they started to sketch out ideas. After a few phone calls they finally met up all in person, albeit it very briefly, at the 'The Hill Country Marathon' outside Austin that Josue was race-directing. On that occasion they only had time to exchange hellos and baseball hats. Allison and Gabe were setting up a tent and promo booth with some swag to give away in the hope of luring in some new clients. The common ground they arrived on was a trip they called Endurance Adventure. Fuego y Agua would supply the endurance - longer runs, mandatory distances to cover, cultural challenges to attempt each day. Rogue would facilitate the adventure - Hamid leading all the on-the-ground logistics in Morocco and Allison's skills to brand and market what was a new product, distinct from their standard trips. They promoted the trip to their respective communities, and even if this new trip sounded like the farthest thing from a relaxing, restorative runcation, a few adventurous souls signed up.

With the trip ideation process with Josue well underway, Allison and Gabe squeezed in some scouting of new and more challenging terrain in the Atlas Mountains during their Morocco trips in Fall 2015. The *piece de resistance* was to be a section of the High Atlas Trail - a rugged a remote high altitude trail through valleys that hid stunning summer sheep pastures and were only accessible by single track trail. Gabe had spotted the start of the trail from the famous road pass of *Tizi'n'Tichka* - the highest road pass in North Africa at over 6000ft, on the way south to the Sahara. "Hey Hamid - where does that go?" He asked, pointed to the ribbon of trail etched into the rocky mountainside which disappeared alluringly around a corner. Hamid did what Hamid does. Made a few calls, charmed a few local goat herders and came away with the names of villages the trail went through. Between trips they hiked the trail with Hamid and it turned out to be one of the most remarkable 30 mile stretches of trail any of them had ever seen. Hidden traditional villages were still only reached by mule tracks. Electricity had only made it in the valleys a few years previous and was still unreliable. The people spoke the local Berber dialect with only basic Arabic. Life was still deeply agrarian. Tending sheep and goats on the tough high altitude pastures and growing alfalfa and wheat on the terraced fields which surrounded the villages. Apple and walnut orchards lined the valley floors were soils where deeper and better watered - everywhere there was evidence of deep and long-lasting understanding of the preciousness of water. The run-off from one terrace carefully turned into the next. Water was made to work and it was slowed and twisted and turned on its way from the melting edge of the snowcapped peaks to the valley floors. Generation after generation had crafted the terraced field to withstand both spring flooding and late summer droughts. For Allison, Gabe and even Hamid - more used to the desert of the south - it was like a trek into a sort of Shangri-La, a land frozen in time and preserved.

Gabe and Hamid marking a 30 mile route through the High Atlas Mountains in Morocco

With this new trail forming the backbone of the trip they were excited for the first Endurance Adventure trip in Spring 2016. It was pushing the boundaries of what had previously been done.

More complicated logistics. More remote trails. More risk in some regards, but every good adventure starts with a step into the unknown. One unknown that Gabe and Allison had not banked on was the guide from the Fuego y Agua side. Shortly before the trip Josue dropped the bombshell that he was out due to personal reasons but assured them, "don't worry, I will send this Irish guy Sean."

Knowing Allison and Gabe as well as I do now I can only imagine the look exchanged and the extended eyerolls when this email came through. Gabe admits with some restraint that he was, "less than impressed." To this point Rogue Expeditions had, to be fair, been doing most of the legwork in terms of preparation for the trip. Now they were getting a guy from the Fuego y Agua side who was not a running guide and had never even been to Morocco. Someone who had not been involved in the planning and design process of the trip very much. Someone who was also pretty elusive when it came to group calls and emails in the immediate run up to the trip. It was an inauspicious beginning.

In my defence, as said Irish guy Sean, the beginning of 2016 was a whirlwind and Morocco got added to occupy pretty much the only free week I had out of the opening months of the year. I was working with the rapidly growing obstacle course events company Spartan Race at the time as they expanded internationally. Country after country I scrambled with local event production teams to stand up new Spartan events. Always just about averting disaster every time in the time-honoured traditions of insane event management hours, unmeetable deadlines, and endless stress everywhere. Winter Spartan events in the Czech Republic and France in January were followed by a dash to Nicaragua for the annual flagship Fuego y Agua event in February. Next up on the Spartan roadshow was Dubai in late February, back to Europe for another winter event in Slovakia, and then back again to the Middle East for Bahrain at the beginning of April. Sandwiched between big events in London one weekend, and Prague a fortnight later, a week running in the High Atlas Mountains in April was, on the whole, mainly a nice excuse to run away from my phone and laptop for a week. I had never heard of a runcation at the time and was more versed in managing the nuances of sufferfest style endurance races for hundreds or thousands of competitors. Nicaragua was my connection to Josue. I lived there for a couple of years between 2012 and 2014 and met Josue on Ometepe where I had fallen off the Central America backpacker trail, found work guiding kayaking and hiking trips, and become happily stuck. He roped me into the world of event management with Fuego y Agua which later led onto Spartan. Morocco would be a departure from the norm, and I had a few misgivings about being so under-prepared going into it, but every good thing in life seems to happen after a little leap of faith into discomfort.

Whatever slight apprehensions, on Allison and Gabe's side as well as mine, might have existed going into the trip, they quickly evaporated when we all met in Marrakech and the universe gave out a satisfying little click. With hindsight it is obvious I suppose that we should be on the same wavelength - we all loved travel, exploring new places, two legs was our chosen mode of transport, and we were all somewhere down the meandering way of what might be called 'alternative career paths'. At the time though runners were arriving so we simply threw ourselves into an action packed week. For the first 3 days we logged long runs with the group in the high desert plateaus just south of the Atlas Mountains, using known Rogue routes and then augmenting them to extend them and make them more challenging. We embedded a group mantra of 'it's not a race' for the runs. We had runners from ultra-running and competitive running backgrounds and so needed to break their habits wanting to race to the finish or get fixated on the pace they were running. It's not a race, slow down, soak in the surroundings, enjoy the miles, there is no winner and no-one is keeping score here. Post run entertainment was on offer every day in order to better immerse the group into the history and culture of the country. A local farmer showed the group how to harvest alfalfa, the standard crop grown to feed animals. Another initiated the group on the back breaking toil of making adobe bricks by hand - the traditional building material of the region. At one of the riads the group had a try at splitting their own firewood and hauling it to heat their showers. Hamid embellished the experience with explanations and storytelling to bring each element into a forming picture of Berber life. On a 21 mile run through the enchanting Todra Gorge, Allison blazed ahead leading the speedsters whilst Gabe and I left the road to clamber up goat trails on the walls of the canyon, both wondering the ever-recurring question of the trail runner: 'I wonder where that trail goes?'

Then on the fourth day we struck out on the High Atlas trail into the wondrous valleys that Allison, Gabe and Hamid had uncovered the previous Autumn. They had retraced the route just days before the group arrived and marked the 30 mile stretch with over 300 hundred pin flags - thin metal stakes about a foot long with a square of red plastic. Feeling sure the way was well-marked I would lead this run as technical single track trails were more my running forte than flat desert or pavement. About 3 of the flags had survived. The other 297 had been upcycled and put to higher purpose by the Berber communities through which we ran. No doubt some of the metal stakes still bind some broken window frames or hold a carrier rack on the back of a motorbike or maintain a satellite dish on an adobe rooftop. The lack of flags made for a rather stressful day of racing around with chalk and ribbon marking arrows and streamers to lure the runners through the valleys. As we passed through tiny mountain villages little children peered out coyly from behind corners and walls, shy as the first runners passed, brazen by the time the last ones came by. *'Bon bon. Dirham, and stilo,'* are the most often requested items from these kids. Sweets, money, and pen. Very clear priorities.

After 11 miles of undulating single track and rugged jeep tracks, through green pastures and along rocky valley slopes, we hit the first road. Hamid awaited with a big smile and some big bundles of firewood. The idea was to add another daily Berber task into the middle of the run. At first we had planned bundles of heavy laundry that the Berber women hauled to and from the rivers most days, but that proved understandably hard to negotiate. Firewood then was the next option. First to arrive, I eyed the bundles in disbelief. Each weighed at least 100 pounds. Tethered with old string and rope. I wrestled with one for a few moments to the amusement of Hamid before dropping it again. I headed on up the trail to keep marking the way. He seemed delighted that we had realistic bundles. Like the local 70 year-old women from the village carried. In theory we would have the runners carry these bundles the remaining 5 or so miles, and 2000 or so feet of climbing, to the remote off-grid gîte we were staying in that night. We did need the wood for heat that night. In Nicaragua in the brutal Survival Run event this task would have been perfectly acceptable punishment. At this moment though we needed the needle slightly more towards the runcation end of the running spectrum. One runner carried the bundle about half a mile - a heroic effort that was enjoyed by most of the local village. The net result of the task was a lot of bonus free firewood for the local village, a lot of hilarity for the local kids, some sore necks and shoulders for the runners who attempted the bundles, and hardcore respect for the Berber grannies who carted these bundles around as a matter of daily necessity.

We exchanged funny firewood stories later that evening in our gîte. The gîte is what this building has come to be called, but I should explain though that it is not a luxurious French country house that the word might conjure up images of. Instead it is a bit damp and cold. It is little more than four walls and a roof. Heated only by a fireplace that puts more smoke into the room than up the chimney. Near the fireplace are a couple of stone benches heaped with blankets and cushions that the whole group piles into and under like mice into hay. Platters of food - ingredients hauled up the mountain on mules by Hamid's team - cooked over a camp stove in the other room arrive for everyone to forage from. Running water comes directly from a stream on the mountain above and is just a tick above freezing in temperature all year round. The toilet flush mechanism is a bucket. The adobe roof is not watertight. On rainy nights you must shuffle your arrangement of blankets around the floor to find a dry patch. But it is a wonderful place. Truly one of the happy places I go to in my mind when I itch to travel.

Getting cozy in the gîte

The night at the gîte was at that sweet spot in a Rogue trip - everyone fully acclimatised, used to the daily routine and engrossed in the running and the travel experience. Everyone in the group had gotten to know each other, shared stories and laughs, and forged a few new memories together. It was not so late in the trip that thoughts had turned to the journey home, or to opening your work email inbox for the first time in a week, or really to any aspect of your life back in the world. We were all living and breathing the experience of that moment. Reliving the 17 tough miles of trail covered that day, the running highs and the sugar bonk lows, the glimpses of village life and insights gained. For a few hours that evening at the gîte it was special. Far from WiFi and phone signal. No music, no television, no Strava to check, no Instagram post to curate. People rotated between stuffing down plates of tasty food, chatting whilst wrapped in blankets by the fire, heading outside on to the terrace for a quiet moment to gaze over the sun setting behind the mountains or later to see the stars fill the night sky. Even I was caught up in it. For a moment forgetting the role and responsibility of guide and just embracing the here and now, the roomful of people and the shared experience. That was probably the moment that I caught the Rogue bug. At the time I wasn't thinking further than the next meal in my life, or perhaps the next event for work at a stretch. But the foundations were laid on that trip, in that gîte, for the next few years of my life.

And we were not done yet. The next day we rose with sounds of village life stirring a few fields away in the small village nearby - roosters crowing, sheep and goats bleating, dogs barking (they had also been at it most of the night), shepherds whistling and yelping as they started the daily move of herd from nighttime enclosure to daytime pasture. We wolfed down a few tagines of Berber omelettes and a few pots of sugary mint tea and toiled over getting socks and shoes onto creaky and stiff legs. Then the weary legs started to cover another 13 miles of High Atlas terrain, weaving through valleys and across high alpine pastures cloaked with scraggly sheep and goats. An occasional shepherd had his splendid isolation punctured by the passing of sportily clad and profusely sweating runners. Their favourite spots to while away the day were betrayed by sooty black rocks against which they liked to brew tea ten times a day or so. One shepherd brought over a freshly born goat kid, still slimy and wet, to one of the female runners - we think it may have been a down-payment on a marriage proposal. After a glorious ridge-line with 360 degree view of mountains and valleys beyond counting, we finally wound down loose rocky trails to a paved road and a waiting minibus. One by one the runners crossed a rickety suspension bridge at the finish, exchanged high fives, buried ice-cold Cokes from the local corner shop (owner startled by the afternoon rush), but quickly realised that euphoria of isolation was over for now. The magic of the gîte was behind. To soften the blow of being 'back in the world' we headed to the mountain town of Imlil, base-camp for adventure tourism in Morocco nestled at the foot of the highest peaks of the High Atlas.

Seen on the run: a shepherd presents Megan with a minutes-old baby goat
Jeff Genova

To cap off what had already been a tough week and a remarkable week, we opted for something tough and remarkable - the highest peak in Morocco, Mount Toubkal rising to 13,617 ft. None of the group had mountaineering skills of note but the idea was one more push to the edge of their comfort zone and a little beyond. They had finished five big days of running, carried firewood, made adobe bricks, learned a few Arabic phrases, observed the traditional agricultural practises up close - in short, they had come a long way along the path of the mountain Berber. Adding the highest peak in Morocco seemed like a fitting end. A final test of mountain toughness. The switch from running to hiking was something of a relief to tired legs but the relief was balanced against colder temperatures and thinner air the higher we trekked up the mountain. The group whittled down a couple of members due to fatigue but the remainder pushed on and made it to the mountain hut at about 10,000ft for a few hours of tossy turny sleep before a very early start on summit day. On the last day of the trip we crept our way up the snowy and icy flank of Toubkal in lockstep with the advancing dawn. Purple and blues turned to yellow and oranges as the sun finally hauled itself above the peaks and we stood on the highest point of North Africa to marvel at it. There is never very much to be said on mountain tops. People tend to mill around wowing to themselves, happy that there is no more up, before realising it is quite cold and a hot shower is a long way away. The long descent transitioned from hiking back to running again as we battered back down the rocky valleys towards Imlil again. A cosy *riad* with hot showers, crackling wood stove, and multi course dinner awaited.

That evening everyone wore the *djellabas* (hooded full length woolen robes fitting for a Jedi) typical of the High Atlas and they tore into the tagines as if they'd been eating them their whole lives. They looked a bit like a table of shepherds after a hard day of drinking tea on a rock. There were a few winces and grimaces as people rose from the table or attempted stairs but it was shared leg pain: group empathy. We concluded dinner with the now customary award ceremony, recognising each participant's contribution to the trip and calling out a few funny stories from the road. We also invited everyone to comment on whether the trip had met their expectations. It was a new concept for us. Back to beta versions and new guinea pigs. The feedback was mostly along the lines of - I didn't know quite what to expect but this exceeded it. It was actually quite hard to summarise and process all they had seen and done in just 7 days. There was a digestion period needed.

From my own perspective I recognised that Allison and Gabe had created a quite brilliant concept, not just this Endurance Adventure but the whole style of what they were doing with Rogue. So much of the fun of the week was organic and seemingly spontaneous - the rambling chats amongst the group over morning coffee or evening tea, or the moments along the trail where we sat on a rock and watched Morocco go by for a few moments, or the interaction with Hamid's driver team during the afternoon drives - their infectious welcome and deep knowledge of their culture and history. Of course the running was brilliant and stunning, the cultural challenges fascinating, the accommodation and the food great - but all that just puts you in a state of readiness to enjoy the experience of really enjoying your travel. I could barely believe that it was only 3 years since the first Rogue trip to Morocco. Allison and Gabe were assured and confident with the place - clearly knowledgeable but understated. They seemed to have answers to every question - meaning behind the names of places, interesting historical details, knowledge about Moroccan cuisine, anecdotes from prior trips that seemed to fit every occasion - and their information came piece by piece in a nice cadence that wasn't forced on the group but sporadically and naturally relayed. Their relationship with Hamid, his family, and his team was unquestionably a special and genuine one - I could feel that, and so could the runners.

It is sometimes hard to formulate your feelings and thoughts after a trip to a place. You have your photographs, perhaps a journal entry, you have a few stories you can tell people off the top of your head. But the deeper details that you absorb from travel are sometimes outside your vocabulary. People talk of getting a sense of a place. Getting a feel for it. We absorb sights and sounds, moments and landscapes, people and interactions - they all get tucked away into our minds but not really in an orderly and retrievable filing system. That's why we crave more though, isn't it? If the sense of place is good, if the soul is fed by a certain travel - the itch returns and you want more. You want to go to the next place, to wonder about the history, to ruminate on the culture, to understand the religion or art or architecture, to admire the landscape in awe, to forge the connections in your mind between one place and another, to see the fundamental commonalities of human experience amidst the kaleidoscope of the world's cultures. We are all, all the people of the world, fascinated by our differences, and by our similarities.

Am I still talking about a running trip, you're wondering? Well yes. But I came away from the trip feeling rather more of a participant than a guide. It brought me back in touch with the 'why of travel' that I had previously known and somewhat forgotten in the midst of endless travel for work. I finished the week like many of the participants - bands of salt crusted on to all my running clothes, socks in a state of toxic nuclear waste shoved deep into the dark recesses of my travel duffel, one or two toenails starting to loom away from their toes in distress, chronically chasing ever more calories despite eating enough for a medium sized family each day, aches and pains in various corners after a hundred or so miles that week, but very happy in that tired and silly sort of way that exertion brings out.

The author on the summit of Jebel Toubkal during his first trip to Morocco, 2016
Jeff Genova

* * *

The year of 2016 saw the addition of the Alpe-Adria trip, the development of the Endurance Adventure idea, and the team grew from two to four with Katie and myself added to the mix. In total Rogue Expeditions did 12 trips and Allison and Gabe had a feeling of increasing stability and confidence in what they were doing. It was 2017 though that the fruits of their labour started to show. In 2017 Allison became a full-time employee of Rogue Expeditions, finally cutting the safety line back to Rogue Running. Indeed Rogue Expeditions as a whole cut the safety line and became an entity in its own right distinct from its sister company Rogue Running, and with Allison and Gabe having ownership. 2017 also saw Gabe earn his first actual pay cheque since leaving his construction job 3 years earlier. One wonders if a time traveller had told him and

Allison that it would be 3 years without actual income in order to build their dream business, would the whole thing have been called off before it started? Perseverance and resilience were starting to pay off. The entrepreneurial roller coaster was finally getting somewhere that was making the ride worthwhile.

These milestones in 2017 were also something of a pausing for breath, a gathering of energy again before any new expansion. No new trips or destinations were added in 2017 - they held steady with Tahoe, Bend, Patagonia, Morocco, Slovenia/Croatia and Kenya. But the groundwork was being laid for new trips all the time. Exploratory calls and email chains. Google documents full of bullet points and links to trails or places to stay or unique selling points. The formula and template were there from the other trips. Now any new destination would have to sit alongside those in a sort of portfolio. Each trip needed to be distinct enough in its own character and storyline. Each needed to have their own imagery and marketing appeal. It was also understood at this point that the success of a new destination was very dependent on the right people, the right network of contacts, and the right level of knowledge of a place. Any new trips needed to appeal to the existing customer base, now growing beyond Austin to include many international participants but still largely US-centric.

One destination that checked all the boxes was South Africa, with a particular eye to the Garden Route along its southwest coast from Cape Town, through the winelands of Paarl and Stellenbosch, to the dramatic coastlines of Knysna and Plettenberg Bay, to the adventure sport hotspot of Stormsrivier, to Port Elizabeth with its nearby big game nature reserves. James Dodds, a coach at Rogue Running in Austin who had been a friend and helper of Rogue Expeditions since the very beginning, had coached a runner called Morgan and she later moved to South Africa to work as a guide for a small family run company focused on outdoor education courses for schools, leadership camps, geography and biology excursions and much more besides. It fitted with what Allison and Gabe has now recognised as their niche - locally owned businesses, smaller scale and hands on, deeply entrenched in the local community, with a lifetime of experience and contacts. Our partners in South Africa, led by husband and wife team Nic and Carma, fit the model beautifully, and were ready to welcome Allison and Gabe to South Africa in late 2017 for a round of scouting.

Before that though there was another iron in the fire. Another place that seemed ready made to fit into the Rogue portfolio - Ireland. Is there any country that Americans love more? Yet startlingly about 50% of visitors to Ireland never make it out of Dublin. We would put that part right. I was about to introduce Allison to the concept of Irish mountain running on the wild and windswept mountains of the west coast.

| 9 |

On Solid Ground: Ireland & South Africa

"I'm pretty sure there is a way down here. The sheep seem to be going this way."

SEAN

One nice thing about being Irish is that, compared with other European nations, we have done relatively little raping and pillaging of other countries. Whilst major European countries were busy drawing lines on maps in places they were not invited to, we were getting bullied by our neighbours, so we wrote poems and songs about that and got drunk. We also stumbled upon the idea that our two major exports to the world were people that could build things and whiskey. Both of which are quite useful and, on the whole, endeared us to the locals when we turned up somewhere. In hindsight this was the foundation of a very successful tourism marketing strategy. Number 1 - don't offend too many people. Number 2 - send out a lot of ambassadors around the world. Number 3 -

mingle. Number 4 - wait for the descendants from Number 2 to come back and visit. Something like 1 in 5 people in the United States claim to have some Irish heritage. This is a startling fact. 60 million people or more with some origin from a country that today has a population of about 6 million if you count the whole island. Catholicism clearly had a role to play in this proliferation. It is also possible that the recent commercial success of the drinking holiday of St. Patrick's Day has played a role in converting a few to the cause (St Patty's Day is wrong folks. No one has ever called it that. Paddy's Day is acceptable. And no one in Ireland eats corned beef. You're welcome.).

In any case the idea of a visit to Ireland is appealing to many Americans. Allison and Gabe had Ireland on their radar for quite a while as a potential trip destination. The fact that Ireland is inherently appealing to their core customer base sat nicely alongside the fact it was relatively straightforward to reach, distinct in its character from the other trips on the Rogue roster, and with my local eye we could come up with something unique even whilst visiting some well-known tourist hotspots. In October 2017, Allison arrived in Dublin for a week of running and planning. By this point in time Katie was embedded into Rogue after her second summer of guiding Run Tahoe and Run Bend, and I had guided the second version of Endurance Adventure Morocco with Allison in March 2017. The team was settling. There was a sense of optimism and forward thinking. A sense that anything was possible. Gabe's spreadsheet forecasts were adding up as the company scaled. He and Allison were now finally earning a living. They were planning and building out the calendar for 2018 and it was looking pretty exciting. Rogue's social media channels and email database were growing at a steady tick. Rogue had been in magazine articles in all the major running magazines and featured on some running podcasts with large audiences. Momentum was building. There was almost a feeling of necessity in adding more trips in order to stay ahead of the demand curve.

From my perspective I was excited to be doing something at home. For the previous 5 years I had been working on running events of various kinds in over 20 countries, but never anything in Ireland. This would be a sort of homecoming and there was a stirring sense of pride that I wanted to make this trip a good one and show Allison the best runs and the best ideas I had. It was also exciting to give more time towards Rogue and carve more time out from my regular job. It was the first time I had been involved in the embryonic first steps of a trip - all the way from blank canvas. We quickly established the trip would focus on Ireland's west coast - catchily renamed in a tourism initiative as the Wild Atlantic Way. The west coast boasts stunning rugged coastlines, picturesque sandy beaches, many of the highest mountain ranges, a feeling of wilderness afforded by low population density, and some of the best preserved traditional culture. All in all exactly the kind of areas that we would like to run through with a group and exactly the kinds of towns and villages we would like to stay in. Perhaps the core appeal of the trip though was indicated by Allison's fondest memories of Ireland. She had visited Ireland for 5 days at the end of a month-long backpacking trip 10 years previously in 2006 after she graduated college. Sure she had enjoyed the scenery and the pub culture and the live music and so on, but most fondly she remembers, "friendly, warm, unpretentious people," that have a flair for welcoming tourists.

With the general area to visit determined, I started to think about runs that we could use for the group and now I ventured into some of the Rogue Expeditions secret sauce ingredients. What makes a good run? Allison had warned me in advance that often only one out of every four runs scouted ended up getting used in a trip. The ideal run is a bit of a Goldilocks story. It wants to be not too long but not too short, not too hard but challenging enough, ideally it features several interesting sights and points of interest but isn't too convoluted and hard to navigate, it should have lots of photogenic moments but not the easily accessible photo spots, it ideally would visit known tourist highlights that we don't want to miss but try to beat the masses by finding a different trail or approach. From a logistics and guiding perspective it is needs to have an accessible start and finish point for vehicles, ideally good phone coverage for communication and runner tracking during the run, and optimally a couple of mobile aid station points where runners can pass a vehicle and grab water or a snack or ditch a coat (or, more likely in Ireland, grab a coat to put on). We need to be able to mark a route for the runners to follow, variously using ribbons, chalk arrows, and flags, ahead of the first runner but then leave no trace and quickly take away the markings after the last runner. Then over the course of the whole trip you want a variety of runs - some on road, some on trail, some mixed surface, some with hills, some more flat, through different terrain types and varying scenery - all adding up to tell a story of the place like a series of chapters.

A couple of days into the scouting trip I had clearly not paid any attention to any of the secret sauce ingredients. I was leading Allison across a boggy open mountainside through whiteout cloud conditions with perhaps 30 feet of visibility. OK maybe it was only 15 feet. We were soaked through from head to toe and had peaty soil coating our legs up to the knees. Allison tells me that prior to this scouting trip she thought 'knee deep in bog' was a figure of speech. Alas not. Goretex hoods up on our jackets, zippers all the way to our noses, and wind buffeting the mountain we couldn't really talk - it was too cold to stop and do so anyway. In theory there was a marvellous view in all directions. We were running along a ridge of mountains that form the spine of the Dingle peninsula in the westernmost tip of Kerry and indeed of Ireland. In theory we could see the Atlantic Ocean on both our left and right, miles distant and hundreds of feet below, and perhaps see mountains and coastline stretching off north and south into the distance. Instead it felt like running through the same 10 yards of bog over and over again in some sort of mirage. Nothing changes. Every direction looked the same. My optimism when we started the run that 'the clouds might lift' was entirely misplaced. The cloud was down and staying down. As it has a habit of doing on the west coast. Most of the year the Northern Atlantic throws weather systems against Ireland's west coast. The prevailing westerly winds bring moist air which rises over coastal hills forming clouds that then dump rain a few miles inland. This cycle almost never ends. So hillwalking and mountain running in Ireland requires steadfast optimism and a very good waterproof jacket.

Run shortly thereafter abandoned, we tried again a day later in the Macgillycuddy Reeks an hour or so drive away. The Reeks are Ireland's highest and most dramatic mountains. Only 3000 feet or so high what they lack in overall height they make up for in ruggedness. Again I was leading Allison along on another of my plotted runs. I had again come up with a theoretical line on Google Earth, combining one or two known trails and then mixing in some open mountain running. It wasn't going well. Again we found ourselves in open boggy terrain with not even a tree or a rock for shelter. To my eye there were obvious sheep paths to follow. To Allison's eye it looked like a wasteland. We hadn't seen anyone all day and there was probably a good reason why. Rain swept sideways in sheets. We slopped and slid along through puddles and sludge. Our feet hadn't been dry in days by this point. Eventually I conceded the route was a bust and was a bit ambitious. I could sense relief in Allison. She was only following me out of necessity at this point. Just to get off the mountains again. I consulted my topo map on my soggy phone screen and decided we should be able to find a route down a steep crag to the road that led through the famous Gap of Dunloe. I pointed off the edge of a cliff into the clouds squinting and hoping to see something that looked like a road below. In hindsight it was a bit sketchy I suppose. Clinging to handfuls of wet grass and heather we scooched and slid and assed our way down the slope. Allison recalls this slope as, "a cliff," adding to confirm her description that this was, "the only moment when I actually thought I might die." Occasionally we passed a wary sheep on a ledge. If the sheep can get down we can get down I declared. Eventually after a few nervy moments, we made it down to the road. Roads are nice, we concluded. They are firm underfoot and provide a good thing to follow. Maybe we should run on roads and not open boggy mountainsides covered in clouds and sheep shit.

On another day we sat in a coffee shop in the town of Doolin, home to the Cliffs of Moher - the dramatic sheer cliffs rising to 700ft above the battering force of the Atlantic waves below. We were drinking another cup of coffee, fiddling on our laptops, repeatedly refreshing the weather forecast apps on our phones, and occasionally squinting out the window into the howling gale force wind and sideways rain for confirmation. Procrastination at its finest. Perhaps late October wasn't the optimum moment for several days of scouting runs. But that was the window we had. Finally, forlornly, we got into running gear and boarded a small shuttle bus that would take us to the trailhead 8 miles away so we could run the length of the cliffs. The bus driver positively beamed at our running clothes. Not another soul was out walking or running. We started running along the cliffs in a sort of 45 degree angle leaning towards the cliff edge to find the balance point in the ferocious wind. We slipped and fell repeatedly. At some point the cliffs formed natural wind tunnels that fully blew us off our feet into stone walls and cattle fences. The waterfalls that usually flowed over the cliffs were inverted - they arched back up on themselves spraying 50 feet into the air, wind rejecting their intention to fall into the ocean below. Yet it was tremendous fun. In the way a child likes to jump in puddles. Sometimes getting soaked by the rain and battered by the wind is exhilarating and revitalising. Even the bog running often has that quality in Ireland. You're running with pretty much zero traction. Just sliding around desperately trying to stay upright, occasionally finding a solid piece of ground, often going to the ankle or knee in the peat and falling headlong. But it can be raw and primal and fun. Humbling and grounding - literally.

Allison getting the full Irish weather experience during a scouting run

After a week or so driving around the west coast we had two trips sketched out. One would be a conventional trip with a mix of road running and a couple of achievable and easily navigable trail runs using existing marked hiking trails. The second trip would be an extension of the Endurance Adventure concept started in Morocco. Some harder, longer and more ambitious mountain runs and some physical challenges that touched on the local culture. With the mountain runs we were again searching for a Goldilocks zone - this time in terms of how lost we wanted people to be or feel. One of our favourite things to tell new groups is that we, "have never lost anyone on a run...Not permanently anyway...At least not yet." Nervous laughter typically follows. It is nice sometimes to feel a bit lost though. It makes you pay closer attention to the landscape. Consider your position and replay where you've just run. Navigating whilst running in mountainous wild terrain makes for a more mindful experience. You're in tune with the passing features of the terrain. Passing through the landscape with understanding rather than mindlessly following markings.

August 2018

A year later with half of the first Run Ireland group missing on a Kerry mountaintop I wasn't really thinking those mindful thoughts though. The runners had slogged their way up Mangerton Mountain, with its commanding views over Killarney National Park and the Macgillycuddy Reeks, to a mountaintop lake called the Devil's Punchbowl. A mile long trail follows the perimeter of the lake, rising over steep, rough, boggy ground as it goes. So far everyone had navigated well, following my markings, so I set a little challenge of sorts. No marking by me from here, just follow the trail around the lake in a full loop and then we will descend back down the trail we came up on. The theory was great. The reality was another version of what happened on the scouting trip. The lake disappeared in the following minutes. Consumed by clouds which quickly billowed in across the mountainside. A few runners managed to finish the loop, wet and windswept, but in high spirits now they had downhill all the way to the finish. A few others got lost in the mirage world of never ending bog and cloud. I trotted around the mountain top and collected them one by one feeling a bit like a chastened sheepdog. In that moment of feeling lost on a mountain top - few people enjoy it. But an hour or two later, freshly showered, gleaming pint of Guinness in front of you in the pub, swapping stories with the other runners, everyone enjoys it. Allison points out that with Irish weather, as frustrating and grim as it can be, she is, "quick to forgive it." A cosy pub, a hearty meal of Irish stew, a roaring open fire, and a whiskey warming your belly - forgiveness for a soaking and battering by the wind comes quick in those conditions.

The first Run Ireland group, warm and cosy in the local pub

It sometimes feels like there is a karmic earning of a good weather day. You must suffer a little in cold and wet in order to reap the reward of a blue sky sunny day where Ireland reveals herself, casting off the shroud of clouds. A pattern emerged with our first two groups in Ireland whereby we got soaked quite often, but then when we really needed the weather it pulled through for us. The groups got to witness the full buffet of possible Irish weather. By having the groups come in late August and early September, the thinking was that there might be a little bit of an 'Indian summer' as the kids go back to school and holiday hotspots quieten down at the end of the summer season. Such theories are all well and good. The reality is that Irish weather is a mixed bag in any month of the year. Yet the Texans in our groups, which still formed the bulk of the runners, were rejoicing in the escape of the oven of Austin to frolic through Irish mist and rain and feel the squelch of mossy ground under their Hokas.

For the second group, our Endurance Adventure crew, they scored blue sky wonderful days just when we needed it most. Good weather blessed their crossing by small ferry to Inisheer, one of the Aran Islands off the coast of Galway and Clare, where they ran a treasure hunt around the island. Using a map they collected Gaelige song lyrics (*Oró, Sé do Bheatha 'Bhaile* - off you go and Google that and try to sing along) from hidden spots around the island before attempting a recital back at the finish line - the local pub. A spot of amusement for the Gaeilge speaking locals who prop the bar up every day. A couple of days later to cap off their trip they again scored a blue sky day whilst we scrambled up Brother O'Shea's gully en route to Ireland's highest peak, Carrauntoohil. Wearing t-shirts and wide smiles they posed for triumphant photos on the roof of Ireland. Stark contrast to the misery a couple of days earlier when we scaled Mount Brandon on the Dingle Peninsula in howling wind, low visibility, and bone chilling sideways rain. You have to earn the good moments. Assigning this kind of karmic reasoning gives one the feeling of playing some part in the weather process. Comforting even if deluded.

A hard-earned clear day on Ireland's highest point

Ultimately though it was the hospitality of Ireland that sealed the trips as a success. Just as it was Allison's lasting memory 10 years on from her first visit, I mused that the things people would remember as the key 'sense of the place' might not necessarily be about the weather and the running. Most likely they would recall the fussy motherlike women in the bed and breakfasts trying to force another sausage into them for breakfast, or the hilarious storytelling boatmen guiding trips on Lough Leane and bouncing stories and legends off our runners so quickly they couldn't distinguish fact from fiction (that's the point), or our local support team Lorna and Ciaran keeping the *craic* (non-drug related fun and laughs - important

Irish word and concept) going even whilst there were some hang-over enforced pit stops during our drives (the risk we ran by having most runs finish at or near a pub each day). I felt a tingle of pride at the Irish sense of welcome. With the eye of an outsider in my own country I can recognise that the level of welcome afforded to tourists in Ireland is a bit unusual. We're actually not always that nice to each other! There is some sort of strange civic pride going on with tourists. Like we all want to make a good impression on the visitors in our house, so let's all be very nice, and easygoing, and good natured, and make sure everyone gets plenty of tea and a good big breakfast.

* * *

"Alright guys, show of hands - who wants to go bungee jumping?"

GABE

November 2018

A couple of months on from those first two Ireland trips Gabe and I flew southbound the length of the African continent from Marrakech to Port Elizabeth on South Africa's Indian Ocean coast. We had just wrapped up another two Run Morocco trips during late October and early November, this time along with Katie for her first Morocco experience. Allison was home in Austin managing the email inbox and social media feeds whilst the other three quarters of the guide team enjoyed another blissful Sahara moment. Gabe and I were planning to do the final scouting tasks of the first South Africa trip by traversing the Garden Route from east to west, finishing in Cape Town, then picking up the group of newly arrived runners and traversing the route from west back to east again. He and Allison had done the initial scouting a year earlier accompanied by Morgan on behalf of our local partners for the trip. They had laid out the broad brush strokes of the trip itinerary - now we had to do the finishing touches. This final snag list is a key part of the process of producing a smooth and successful trip. You need to start planning about 12 months in advance of a trip in order to meet the lead time for permits, sales and marketing, reservations for accommodation and other logistics. But so much can change in those 12 months that you really need another look on the ground closer to go-time. Gabe was in significantly better health than his scouting trip a year previous with Allison. Most of his stories from the 2017 scouting trip stemmed from a little gift of our old friend *Ouagadougou* that followed him from Morocco, where he and Allison had just guided trips (he points the finger at Allison as the carrier, she claims evidence is inconclusive). "Hours and hours spent in the toilet of an Airbnb apartment," Gabe recalls in dejected memory. They had hiked Table Mountain when he was sufficiently recovered but he was still weak, sweating, and stopping often to sit on rocks in the shade. "My memory is that I was still sick - buuuuuut Allison *assured* me that I would be fine," he offers here - I'm fairly confident he didn't love the hike. After this, they had rented a car to do further scouting after an all-day convoluted rental car process he summarised as, "a complete clusterfuck." Sometimes travel is like that. It seems to fight you at every turn. And you end up driving a stick-shift on the wrong side of the road as a reward.

So it was certainly the case with South Africa that we needed another look. There were still details to finalise and some hurdles to overcome. In 2018 Cape Town suffered through the worst drought in its history so we waited anxiously as the trip crept closer and the city reserves of freshwater ominously counted down day by day. The story gained international news attention, framed as a foreshadowing of things to come around the world as the problems of climate change and population growth progressed. At one point it seemed sure we would cancel the trip. Tourism simply isn't ethical in such a context. But rains arrived and the situation eased just in time although many water saving measures endured in the city and became cultural norms - quick showers, even quicker hand washing, use of greywater from your sink or shower to flush your toilet, amongst others.

We encountered other issues on our journey westward from Port Elizabeth. Huge swathes of forest and mountainside had been consumed by forest fires near Stormsrivier, Knysna and other places along the coast. The black scarred countryside was sobering to drive through and we crossed some areas of the Tsitsikamma National Park off the list of potential running locations and found replacement routes. We made it to Stellenbosch to meet with our local partners for the trip, husband and wife team Nic and Carma Shaw. They were immediately warm and welcoming and struck me as easy and interesting conversationalists. Nic's knowledge on all things South Africa was astonishing and one topic ran into the next as our planning meeting threatened to become a cultural roundtable. Carma however was armed with a folder of trip info and I knew she meant business when it opened and Nic went quiet in deference. Riddled with post-it notes and sectional dividers, the folder was a bible of reservations, timings, things to double check, things to triple check, contact information, estimated drive time durations, dietary restrictions, and preferred choice of beer. OK maybe not the beer, we could improvise that bit, but otherwise the next nine days of our lives were planned.

A pre-trip meeting of the minds in Nic and Carma's office in Stellenbosch, South Africa

As we went through final planning and logistics they added yet another curve ball. Several trails both in the Table Mountain National Park and the so called Fisherman's Trail from Hout Bay to Fish Hoek had been designated unsafe by the park rangers following a robbery of hikers a few days prior. Another one of our running routes was torpedoed and another thing to worry about was added. Outbreaks of 'bandit attacks' on trails are a recurring problem in the Cape Town area with big signs at trailheads warning 'only hike in groups' and 'don't carry any valuables.' If you manage to dodge the bandits there are still baboons to worry about - they can be an aggressive menace on trails and have been known to attack people even if not very often. A day later we went trail running with Nic in the stunning Jonkershoek National Park near Stellenbosch about an hour out of Cape Town. Along the way he warned us there were many danger noodles (snakes) to worry about, from Cape Cobras to Black Mambas, from Puff Adders to Boomslangs - all of which are capable of delivering a fatal bite to a clumsy trail runner. The onus would be on the lead guide to keep their eyes peeled and turn back rather than pass any snake that might be lying on a trail warming itself. Gabe, with long experience of Texas rattlesnakes was rather more confident than me from harmless snake-free Ireland. There were nasty plants to avoid that could sting and scratch and tear at bare legs and even leopards to think about - Nic was overwhelming us at this point, was he still serious? He was. Although the Cape Leopards are relatively small and attacks on humans are very unlikely due to their shyness. In general Nic isn't in the habit of joking on these kinds of matters. An active member of the mountain rescue community Nic has a deep knowledge, fascination almost, with search, rescue, and first aid in adventurous emergencies. His practical experience and advice, along with Carma's flair for organisation and logistics, made for a solid team to rely on.

More than ever Gabe and I were acutely conscious in our role as the responsible tour guides. Guides are there to understand the situation, to evaluate it, and to mitigate risk. In the adventure tourism case to which we belonged, the guide is there to bring clients into a situation that they might not go into alone. The guide should manage and facilitate a safe experience, even if the client perceives risk. This perceived risk is often the point - the whole sense of adventure is going beyond the usual comfort zone. The guide draws on thousands of hours spent in the given adventure context - from trail running to mountain climbing, from ziplining to deep-sea diving - to ensure the activity goes on within safe parameters. To call a halt if the parameters are exceeded, and to be the safety net and insurance policy if accidents or emergencies do happen. It seems to me there could almost be a tour guide's oath along these lines. A code of conduct. For our small niche within the adventure tourism world we forged our own path. Committing to paper emergency action plans, detailing nearest medical facilities, keeping our first aid and wilderness medicine skills and training up to standard, inventorying our first aid kits that were carried on-trail, adding fall back plans and turnaround points in case of bad weather, additional layers of logistics support, checking and re-checking the plan endlessly until confidence levels were good and contingencies were solid.

Plans in place, logistics all set, we had a couple of days to recharge our batteries before the group arrived into Cape Town. Besides finalising emergency actions plans, studying snake ID charts and snakebite first aid protocols, Gabe and I had some other very important business to attend to. Guide downtime. We had been on the go non-stop for four weeks straight at this point with back to back trips in Morocco and then the days traveling and scouting between Port Elizabeth and Cape Town. Decompression and energising are an important part of the process if you're to be in good form for a newly arriving group. So we checked into an Airbnb apartment in Stellenbosch and set about perfecting the guide downtime routine. All your crusty running laundry (there is a finite limit to how many times you can turn things inside out) needs to be washed and dried (formula for quantity of running socks and underwear = number of days of trip plus one). With solid WiFi finally attained one needs to review all the unread emails and answer some small percentage of them to buy some extra time until an actual office day. Then power down your brain and utilise the WiFi to disappear into a Netflix series for a few hours - nothing too mentally demanding. Something nice and fluffy and light. Often viewed from the floor whilst contorted over a foam roller or trigger point ball. A large quantity of snacks must be procured - any kind of comfort food. Ideally salty after weeks of hot weather sweaty running

- in my case every possible flavour of Kettle Chips available and a share bag of salted pistachios. Survey local restaurants for yet more comfort food - thankfully Stellenbosch was a jackpot of craft beer, tacos, and sliders. Review several weeks of news headlines and social media - quickly realise you haven't missed much. Complete obligatory phone calls to wife/husband/girlfriend/boyfriend/family to demonstrate you're still alive. Verbal communication between guides during this period is typically at an absolute minimum. Bear in mind guides share a room for weeks on end and whilst guiding a group are 'on' for days on end so can be pretty much talked out by the end of a trip. This whole process typically takes 48 hours and is a tried and tested procedure. Bright eyed and bushy tailed we headed into Cape Town for the arrival of the group.

In the space of the following nine days we crammed in as much of the Garden Route as is humanly possible with the group. First up, in Cape Town we scaled the imperious Table Mountain from one side, ran over the top, and descended down another flank to an awaiting 'lekker' picnic in the city's beautiful Kirstenbosch Botanical Gardens. Carma laid on the five star picnic of delicacies and 'lekker' an Afrikaans word meaning superb or fantastic which can be applied equally to a person, object or event, was added to the growing essential South African vocabulary alongside 'howzit' - how is it going, 'just now' - not now, but quite a bit later than now, and 'is it?' - response to most questions, roughly equating to really?

We scored a perfect weather day on Table Mountain which is so often draped in cloud. To begin with views of the rocky outcrop of Lion's Head punching through the early morning mist nearby, then ocean views were revealed on all sides whilst on the plateau at the top, then came views over the city on the descent. A tough, challenging run for the first day out, but a rewarding one. The group had time to check out the main sites of Cape Town and even visit

Robben Island, the island prison made famous by Nelson Mandela. Nic was quickly filling the 'Hamid role' with ready knowledge of South Africa's fascinating if often troubled history and demonstrating an impressive command of *Xhosa*, - all the difficult mouth clicks included - one of ten official languages of the country.

A picture perfect day on top of Table Mountain in Cape Town

The next day the rains came down in Africa. Given the stress of the water shortage in the lead-up to the trip it was almost inevitable we would get soaked on the run along Cape Town's waterfront to the stunning sandy beach at Camps Bay. Despite the rain a few runners finished with a dip in the ocean - the Atlantic, to be followed later in the trip with Indian Ocean swimming. Before leaving the Cape area we added the obligatory tourist stop at Boulders Beach to see the world's most northerly penguins hanging out on a sandy beach in a warm country looking very out of place. A snake-free run in Jonkershoek followed the next day, with Nic pointing out many interesting Fynbos plants belonging to the Cape plant kingdom (the only plant kingdom in the world solely contained in one country - fascinating principally as every plant you see is almost certain to be new to you as it doesn't exist anywhere else in the world), and then a visit to one of the many vineyards for an afternoon (and evening) of excellent wine-tasting. Next we veered off the coast to stay at a vast sprawling ostrich farm that had flavours of Montana's big sky country - huge rolling prairies meeting wide open skies. Dramatic sunrises and sunsets. Dusty roads and very few people. We spent the night on the farm in splendid isolation and the next morning for breakfast had the novelty of choosing either ostrich or chicken eggs for our omelettes.

Back on the coast again we ran a beautiful trail at Mossel Bay that really captures most the great features of the Garden Route coast - craggy cliffs, stunning sandy beaches, thundering roar of the waves, ever changing but ever stunning vistas of the ocean, fresh coastal breeze keeping temperatures comfortable even in steady sunshine, dassies (rock hyraxes, similar looking to a marmot) hopping away in surprise as you turn each corner, all in all dreamy trail running. We even squeezed in some early evening whale watching and dolphin spotting to round off the day. The next couple of days crammed more in with time exploring the stunning little peninsula of Robberg Nature Reserve, an impossibly picturesque place, where it feels like you are moving through a series of postcards of beach and ocean scenes. We followed this with some great running in and around Stormsrivier through beautiful, forested trails and along the craggy rock-hopping trail right on the ocean's edge called the Otter Trail - one of South Africa's most famous.

The most memorable moment from that first group was probably late afternoon on a drive near Stormsrivier when Gabe called the bungee jumping centre at Bloukrans Bridge. He announced to the minibus of tired runners that there was time for a bungee jump, but they literally had 60 seconds to decide whether to reserve a spot and we would be at the bridge in 10 minutes to do the jump. At first they thought he was joking. Laughing off his phone call as staged, and then the expressions changed to 'wait, what - is he serious?' The bungee at Bloukrans is pretty close to the top of the list of the highest bungee jumps in the world. The jump takes place from the underside of the huge arched road bridge that passes over the yawning 700ft deep gorge. So high you can barely make out the river in the distance below. We had previously mentioned the jump teasingly to the group but left the final decision open and spontaneous - now the moment was upon them. One of the runners Kimberley shot her had up and said she was in. No other takers though. Fear of heights and an assortment of running injuries under management kept the numbers low. "3 reservation please," Gabe informed the reservation desk - naturally being the caring and conscientious guides that we are, we had better jump as well.

There really isn't any way to adequately describe the initial freefall seconds of a bungee in words. It is just an alternative type of sensation where your brain is left behind and takes a few minutes to catch up and produce the adrenaline, the yelps, the wows, and the 'holy shit - did that just happen' feeling. We may have been a little giddy for the remainder of the drive that evening. If bungee jumping was a more modern addition to the list of traditions in South Africa, we followed with a more time-tested one - a 'braai' - the Afrikaans word for grilling which typically refers to a communal barbecue meal. South Africans like to put all manner of meats on the grill. No animal is safe from the menu, from impala to kudu, from crocodile to ostrich. We stuck to mostly conventional choices (along with some veggie and vegan options) but even so it made for an ideal evening of beer drinking around the fire cooking meat on sticks in the tradition of a thousand generations before us.

It was hard to top that *braai* evening and everything that went before but with the final day of the trip we gave it a shot. We stayed at a stunning thatched farmhouse that had been converted into a swanky safari-feel guesthouse with Africana art on the walls, traditional music and dance performances in the evening, and in-house safari drives to nearby Addo Elephant Park at dawn and dusk. It was a departure from the feel of the Garden Route and a taste of another part of South Africa's appeal. Addo has played a critical role as a sanctuary for the region's elephants - rescuing the population from just 11 around the time of its founding in 1931 and hauling it to over 600 today. The park has exciting plans to expand and merge with marine and coastal nature reserves - this would make it a world first for seeing the 'Big 7' - adding whale and great white shark to the land based 5. It was nothing less than exhilarating to see elephants, zebras, hartebeests, warthogs, cape buffalo, kudu, impala, and even a lioness up close. We even squeezed in another safari drive through the park on our way to Port Elizabeth airport - luggage and all loaded in the truck! If that wasn't a South African moment to end the trip then I don't know what is.

"We keep finding the right kind of people," muses Allison thinking back on the initial scouting of South Africa and the trip that came together in conjunction with Nic and Carma and their team - initially Morgan and later their other employees Callum and Dale. One after another interesting and competent, dependable and knowledgeable. Finding the team to put together a week of experiences like the previous few paragraphs outline is really the key. With the right people and the right planning, it all goes off smoothly, but only after an investment of group brain energy. Several months of thinking and tweaking for several days of packed action. A sliver of South Africa's geography explored but a deep dive taken into the place, the story, the history, the people, and of course the running.

Allison returned with Gabe to guide South Africa again in 2019. The trip stands out to her for the number of nationalities that made up the group. Long gone by then were the days of a dozen Austinites making up the group - Australia, Italy, Ireland, UK, US, Canada and South Africa were all represented in the group. The most international group yet. People were finding their way into Rogue groups from ever more distant places. Besides geographic spread, the typical Rogue Expeditions runner at this point was hard to also pin down - we had people from their 20s up to their 70s, from solo travellers to groups of friends to couples, from elite runners to 'run/walk' style runners just starting out, from people who got their very first passport for a Rogue trip to seasoned travellers who had seen the world already. By the end of 2018 and the beginning of 2019 trips were selling out quickly and people were finding Rogue Expeditions by all manner of means that Allison and Gabe couldn't have imagined a few years prior. Marketing and spreading the word is like that. Eventually it takes on a whole organic momentum and life of its own. Tendrils of connections spread out and away. Every marketing email, every social media post, every business card handed out, every poster in a running store, every pop-up tent at a marathon event, every dollar spent on search engine optimisation and Facebook advertising - all adds up to an impression made on the world of runners and travellers. New runners got added to a growing community trip by trip and mile by mile. Led by us of course, but not entirely - it was also taking on a life of its own led by the alumni runners who were on their fourth or fifth or sixth destination by this point - the evangelicals. They were often the ones to make an impact on new runners with their stories (without encouragement or bias from the guide team!) from their other trips and their familiarity with us helped form the right kind of group atmosphere we sought to build with new groups. The community growth was also fostered and encouraged by a supportive online community sharing posts and news and stories and pictures from their own trips. The 'a-ha' moment in terms of growth arrived with the announcement of our next new trip - Run British Columbia. Announced with minimal fanfare, a few short lines of text description and a few pics of forested mountains, we had 12 runners signed up for it within 45 minutes of launching the registration page. Long forgotten were the anxious days in the RV when the dreaded Squarespace notification of a person cancelling their reservation came through.

British Columbia had a number of the elements we were looking for in adding a new destination. It had the raw and rugged appeal of amazing nature, in the same way that a place like Patagonia has. Yet it was quite accessible with direct flights to Vancouver from most places in the US - with so many faraway destinations on our trip roster an additional 'closer to US' trip was appealing. It had very established tourist destinations like Whistler or Squamish that would have lent themselves to a potential trip but it also had huge chunks of lesser explored territory and that was exciting and enticing. We already had a key piece of the puzzle in that we had a contact up north who worked in the outdoor adventure space, was a keen trail runner, and was very interested to partner up to produce a trip. It was time for another scouting trip.

Runners from seven different countries making up the most diverse group yet in 2019

| 10 |

Survival Skills: British Columbia

"You know how to tell grizzly bear shit from black bear shit, right?"

FRASER

September 2018

S andwiched between the first Ireland trips and the beginning of the Morocco and South Africa guiding spell, I settled in for a flight from Dublin to Vancouver with a heroic hangover. Meeting a friend for 'just a couple of pints' is a sort of a lie that Irish people tell themselves, equivalent to the runner who pledges an early morning run tomorrow - 100% sure, no doubt this time, no backing out - only to ignore the alarm again and pull their duvet over their head. The couple turned into at least a dozen and pulling a duvet over my head was exactly what I wanted to do. Instead I suffered through 10 hours of dehydrated purgatory and vowed repeatedly to stay clear of Temple Bar next time. Another thing Irish people lie to themselves about. The pain didn't ease as I deplaned and made my way into the thronged immigration hall in Vancouver airport. There was no escape - the queue wound forward in an endless snake of which I couldn't even see the end. One hour of queueing turned interminably into three before I finally escaped, rushed to collect my luggage, and sprinted to the bus connection to the domestic terminal. I needn't have rushed - I arrived a few minutes after the departure of the only flight of the day to Bella Coola, a small coastal town an hour's flight north about halfway up the vast province of British Columbia. There are those moments when traveling when you just want to curl up on top of your luggage, give up, and sleep it all away. Instead I regrouped, rebooked, found WiFi, found a cheap room to stay in, hunted for food and fluids like a feral dog, and then crashed early for the night.

In hindsight I am glad I was fresh and awake for the flight to Bella Coola - it was like no flight I've ever taken before. A small 19 seater plane cruised low, just over innumerable snowcapped peaks with huge sinuous glaciers flowing between them, before banking down into a deep forested valley, the treetops seemingly very close beneath us, and bumping to a halt on a strip of tarmac nestled in the forest. I closed my mouth for the first time in an hour, hopped off, and proceeded to the terminal building - about the size of a modest bungalow. The guy who had waved the plane into its stand position was now pushing a cart to the plane to retrieve the luggage. He was a one man airline - managing reservations, check-in process, baggage handling, plane parking, and on cloudy days cycling around the runway whilst on the phone to incoming pilots to tell them where a hole in the cloud might be. I immediately loved it all.

Waiting to pick me up was my friend Luis Escobar who had arrived a couple of days earlier. "Fraser is pretty busy," he reported referring to Fraser Koroluk whom we were both here to visit and stay with. The three of us were connected by the same ultra-marathon event in Nicaragua that had in a roundabout way connected me to Rogue. Luis is a pillar of the ultra-running world widely known as one of the best photographers in the business and also for organising his own unique running events near his home in California. Fraser is a Bella Coola local but, as with many Canadians, a swallow who liked to migrate south in the winter - preferring to drive his campervan to California or fly down to Nicaragua seeking warm weather and cheap beers once the tourism season ended in the Fall. The three of us had at various points in the preceding years met up in Nicaragua or California for acts of long distance running.

As Luis drove me back to Fraser's cabin, as he called it, he asked me with a mischievous grin if I was really here to do 'a bunch of running.' Of course I said - I'm here to scout a new trip. His eyebrows rose high with the next sentence, "there are *a lot* of bears around." It is hard to talk about Fraser or about Bella Coola and not talk about bears. Fraser and his father Les have been guiding nature tours on the rivers of Bella Coola valley for decades. The star attraction are the grizzly bears in the Fall when they gather in the salmon filled rivers for a feast before winter comes in. Fraser is a fish biologist by training and would much rather talk about the reproductive cycles of salmon, but the paying tourists want to see the big hairy things eating the salmon. So he has spent thousands of hours rafting slowly and gently past feasting bears, with photography tourists and nature lovers filling his raft, and asking him in hushed awe the same dozen questions day after day. How much does a bear weigh? How long is a bear's pregnancy? How dangerous are they really? What do they eat when there are no salmon? How long do they hibernate for? It is understandable therefore, that when he finishes work for the day, the last topic he wants to talk about is bears. But I just so happened to have an awful lot of bear-related questions. Especially as it was clear no-one was going to be joining me on any runs.

Luis and I settled into Fraser's cabin - well, Luis settled in. He had claimed dibs on the spare room in the small wooden cabin. I started stringing my camping hammock between two trees outside. Luis's eyebrows went up again, *a lot.* As I set up my hammock I soaked in the surroundings. The cabin was set amongst towering cedar trees. From the front deck of the cabin one could gaze up the south wall of the valley, a couple of thousand feet high, and see several waterfalls tumbling down amongst a patchwork of stubborn trees that clung to the steep slopes. On the northside of the valley a mosaic of huge rock faces, hundreds of feet high, were peering out from wispy clouds and fog. A hundred yards or so behind the cabin through the trees I could hear the rumble of the Bella Coola river. This was real nature - big and bold. Fraser came striding across the lawn area that separated his cabin from his rafting tours workshop and office. He looked exactly like a grizzly bear tour guide should look like - unruly long greying hair flowed out from under a baseball cap, a scruffy beard completed the look along with obligatory khaki tour guide shirt and wader style waterproof trousers and braces. In his hand was a bag of what looked suspiciously like several beer cans. It was 5 o'clock in Bella Coola it seemed. I winced - I could still count the number of hours since my hangover symptoms had receded but resistance was futile. "I've been waiting years for a visitor," Fraser announced, "and now I have two at once," popping open three cans. He stooped and peered underneath the raised cabin, "has anyone seen Monkey?" He enquired. "My cat - she doesn't like visitors. Let's leave the cabin door open for the next couple of days in case she wants to come in." Almost on queue some dogs started barking nearby through the forest. I looked questioningly towards the kerfuffle. "Just a bear," Fraser shrugged and went inside leaving the door wide open. Unnerved, head full of thoughts of hammock bear entanglement, I accepted the beer and filed away all questions of bears. Perhaps ignorance really is bliss.

It became clear that Fraser really was as very busy as Luis had indicated. Mid-September was peak bear viewing season. He was booked out doing two tours a day, early morning and late afternoon, seven days a week. Luis was accompanying him with his camera gear on several tours to take a variety of marketing shots. Every day brought different weather and different bears on different sections of the river. So I would be left to my own devices for scouting some running routes. Ideally I would have come in the summer, June or July, whilst the weather was better, the days longer, and the grizzly bears were up in the high alpine terrain far away from most the trails I would be running. As it happened, September was the only option in order to line a trip up for Summer 2019 so it was now or never.

The next morning over very early coffee Fraser hurriedly threw facts and bear spray at me. "Keep this in your running pack," he said passing the deodorant sized red can, "instructions are on it." Next he passed the keys to his 4x4 Dodge truck - "ignore all the warning lights on the dash," he explained, "it is old but working fine." I leafed quickly through some maps of the local area and asked again about which areas he liked to run in most. He pointed them out but almost every trail came with some caveat - watch out for logging work here or watch out for a washed out forest road there. "Bears will generally only be in the rivers or nearby rivers," he added. I glanced at the maps again - *all* of the trails seemed to be beside rivers. "What about a bear bell?" I inquired, holding up the little bell I had found in the cabin. I was pretty sure this was just a toy for Monkey and that Fraser had never in his life utilised it as a warning bell for bears. "You know how to tell grizzly bear shit from black bear shit, right?"

Fraser asked with a laugh. "Grizzly bear shit has the bear bells in it." I would hear this joke from every single person I met in Bella Coola in the next week - they really seemed to enjoy it. "You should be fine," he said on his way out the door. *Should be*, I thought? He paused, "you have a satellite communicator, right? You won't have any phone signal all day." Yes I confirmed. "Yeah should be fine," he repeated. Luis followed him, one last raised-eyebrows nod in my direction before he left.

Grizzly print by the river

Thoughts of hammock bear entanglement were now replaced by thoughts of trying to type out a message on my slow and clunky Delorme satellite communicator whilst under any kind of bear related duress. Nonetheless I packed my running bag, laced up my trail running shoes, and headed off exploring in Fraser's truck. About

10 minutes into the drive, along a gravel logging road that climbed away from the valley floor, I crossed a bridge - literally the first river I crossed. I slowed the truck and glanced out the window - there about 50 feet away in the middle of the river a very large hairy salmon-eating animal glanced back at me. It is a funny feeling when a grizzly bear looks at you. It is like they don't really see you. No surprise or panic or sign of alertness. They almost look through you. They register your presence coldly and calmly and they then continue their bear-related business. You're irrelevant to them. As long as you stay out of the way. The bear padded off down the slippery rocks. I drove the other direction further up the valley. After this rather worrying start I set off running and made regular calls of 'hey bear' into the quiet of the trail ahead. In spitting rain under a grey sky I ran to a lookout point at a col amongst the mountains that peered across towards Purgatory Glacier which hung off mountains across a huge valley before me. The tongue of ice was a clue to what lay beyond the mountains in that direction - the Monarch Icefield, over which I had flown on the way in, a vast expanse of ice punched through by countless peaks, a true wilderness area where few venture. I doubled back and ran downhill including possibly my fastest mile ever run after a loud and worrying rustle in the bushes alongside the trail. Near the truck I paused to admire Odegaard Falls, a stunning waterfall, and the surrounding trails that wove through the quiet forest. I hadn't seen a single person or a single vehicle all day. Just one natural wonder after another.

This run was the beginning of an overriding sense in the next days that the areas around the Bella Coola valley were real nature. More 'real' than I had experienced before. More raw, more natural and untamed. The forests were bigger and older and stirred ancient emotions, the mountains were too wild for recreation, the glaciers and icefields were too inhospitable for exploration except by the very experienced. Bears, wolves, moose, and caribou still roamed the landscape at will. Even the people seemed to have an almost frontier existence. Backyards were full of junk and scrap metal - every tool and item would have a use in time. The supermarket was more of a wholesale provision store selling bulk quantities of everything from daily groceries to hunting equipment, fishing tackle and power tools. The 2000 or so people that called the Bella Coola valley home were a mixture of the indigenous *Nuxalk* people and descendants of more recently arrived Norwegian immigrants. In spite of their differences, to me they all seemed similar in their understanding of the wild place they lived and the multi-purpose skillset that one needs to flourish in it. Everyone needed to be their own carpenter, mechanic, welder, stonemason, machine operator, hunter, fisherman and farmer. One day Fraser would be out in the community stringing up electric fences around apple trees to deter bears from intruding and the next day he had stories of a helicopter flight up to the icefield to make an aerial inspection of a glacier they were worried would calve off and cause a flood surge on the river - just another Tuesday. This wasn't a run of the mill existence.

That evening Fraser laughed off my panic at the rustle in the bushes during my run as, "probably just a black bear." Although smaller and generally less threatening than grizzlies I still didn't fancy running into a black bear engrossed in its berry hunting. He seemed to be dodging my questions about whether he often met bears whilst he was out running or how common it was to have aggressive bears in and around the community. Instead he invited me for a couple of river floats in the coming days to see the bears up close in their natural habitat doing their thing. Seen this way, from a respectful distance, it helps to diffuse some tension and replace it with some understanding. Gradually in the following days I got more and more comfortable alone in this wilderness setting and a picture of the running adventure we could offer here came together. Together with Fraser initially, and then with Allison and Gabe in the weeks after my initial scouting, we stitched together an itinerary that captured the richness of the area. Combining the appeal of remote wilderness with the comfort of homely lodges, we pieced together complicated logistics that only made sense for a bigger group, incorporated the various landscapes and terrains available - the 'Great Bear Rainforest' landscape of the coastal valleys and the wide open expanses of the Chilcotin Plateau 4000 feet above and 60 miles inland, fitted in canoeing and rafting, and of course a whole suite of runs.

We had an itinerary - what I didn't have though, were good pictures. It rained on every single run I went on. I had dozens of dank, grey, gloomy pictures. Cloud shrouded spruce trees and mountain sides that disappeared into fog. Later in the scouting trip up on the plateau above the valley I ran into considerable early winter snow and had to abandon a couple of runs. Pictures from those runs were white on white. We knew by this point that pictures were our most important asset in telling the story of our trips online. Good running pictures drive interest. By 2018 Instagram had emerged as the core tool for this storytelling. Facebook was becoming more of a utility - a place to post photo albums, create private groups for runners to meet and contact each other, a place for digital marketing - but not really an effective storytelling tool (Twitter was a place to avoid for the sake of your sanity). For Instagram, we had even come up with a magic formula for the best running pictures. The harsh reality is that all the best pictures were staged. We called it the 5 S's of Rogue running pictures. The formula was created by another great running photographer Jeff Genova who had joined us on the first Endurance Adventure Morocco trip. We would explain these early in a trip as part of our 'run talks' when we huddled pre-run to give a few directional pointers for the day, some history or info about the area we were running and so on. The 5 S's go as follows:

When you see a run guide stick a phone in your face during a run, get ready to 1. Smile - a nice big toothy smile even if you are grimacing on the inside and your thighs are chafing. 2. Shoulders back - get that posture in shape, shoulders back and chest out - just create the illusion you have a nice lithe running gait for a moment, then you can hunch over and get back to the grind. 3. Swing - get those arms nice and loose and swing them with each stride - you'll look like Usain Bolt cruising for the finish line rather than a mile 20 marathoner looking like they are having a seizure. 4. Stride - lengthen that stride out - just pretend you're a graceful gazelle gliding over the ground rather than the flat footed shoe dragging shuffler we know you usually are. 5 - Suck it in. Self-explanatory. Get that core nice and tense for a couple of breaths - you may get some dating app profile pic material here after all. Gabe usually liked to add a bonus number 6. Silly - do whatever silly shit comes into your head. Those random and silly pics are usually solid gold. As guides were often doing the bulk of the photography, we ran around like demented sheepdogs back and forward though the pack of runners getting the right angles in front of the good views then getting back to the front or back of the pack again. Without runners to take pictures of, and with the weather hiding the landscape for the duration of my stay, it was all the more amazing that we sold out the 12 spots for the first Run BC trip on the back of one or two social media posts (with gloomy mysterious pictures) and a teasing promo email that was mostly written description. It felt incredibly vindicating that there was a high level of trust building from our clientele - they figured that if we were going running in some remote area of British Columbia that they had never heard about, it'd be good. There would be a good reason. They would follow.

Anna perfectly demonstrating the 5 S's in the Bella Coola Valley

* * *

"End-of-trip high fives have been outlawed ever since."

ALLISON

July 2019

I awoke in a bit of a panic from a light sleep in my camping hammock. The rain was still drumming incessantly, as it had been doing for over 24 hours straight, on the tarp I had strung the hammock under. Another noise woke me though - a massive deep rumble further up the valley from the campsite. I swung out my hammock, clicked on my headtorch, checked the time at 2am and walked a few yards out to the floating pontoon on Turner Lake, set deep into the wild landscape of Tweedsmuir National Park, and peered into the rainy night. The rumble was a landslide, I was pretty sure about that, nothing else could account for such a noise. I had visions of a rain-triggered mud and rock landslide ploughing into the shallow alpine lake we were camped beside. A surge wave down the lake would follow surely. I watched and waited for a few minutes. Everyone else in camp seemed to be fast asleep still. I returned to my hammock feeling a little sheepish. Maybe I was getting a little too into this whole wild country thing.

Next morning I reported my midnight rambling to Fraser.

"Oh yeah?" He replied in the age old Canadian tradition of answering a question without really answering it and still being polite at the same time. He was dismissing my nonsense. Slowly the rest of our camp roused out an assortment of simple wooden cabins and tents and headed for the morning coffee pot. Allison and I were over the halfway point of guiding the first ever Run BC trip. We were based at a remote wilderness camp for two nights, in what we had billed as the high point of the trip. Despite it being mid-July the rain hammered down and the temperatures were decidedly chilly. We had visions of lake swimming under blue skies (based on the weather Allison and I had just a week earlier in our last scouting run before the group arrived), carefree evenings around the campfire, impromptu jogs and hikes to nearby beauty spots, and lots of canoeing. Instead we were swaddled in Goretex, huddled under tarps, drinking hot drink after hot drink, feverishly feeding the campfire, and listening to one of the runners Michael read aloud from a bear book he had brought along. And yet it was still a high point of sorts. Much like the gîte was in Morocco, this was a special place. Just to be here, in spite of the weather, was a gift. The runners had slogged their way through more than 10 miles of tough trail with about 4000 ft of ascent and then canoed 2 miles along the lake to reach the spot. Our food and camping supplies were flown in a small supply plane that could land on the lake. The plane, a Canadian built de Havilland Beaver, was itself a part of the history and culture of remote BC life having rolled off the production line 70 years previously but still flying supplies to backcountry fishermen, hunters, and now trail runners. There is off the beaten track, and then there is this camp spot. Way out there. Off grid in the wilderness. Loons sounded their weird but charming call around the lake, forests and mountains stretched away to each horizon. There wasn't another human for miles around. Those who love the outdoors know these kinds of places. Our souls yearn for these wild intact ecosystems - we feel it in our bones.

In another parallel to the Morocco gite, it was getting to the nice part of the trip for group bonding. We had all gotten to know each other. The storytelling was getting into the adult variety and the joke telling was progressing into the inappropriate. The runners in this group had somewhat self-selected so as to be nature enthusiasts who were comfortable with a couple of days 'roughing it' in a wilderness setting. The group were all in the groove of carrying bear spray and a bell on runs, typically running in pairs or small groups, and generally making plenty of rumpus as they made their way through the forested trails around Bella Coola - better to be nice and loud so all the animals can hear you and get out of the way, and there really weren't any other tourists to disturb. On the topic of no other tourists - that had been the way of it for several days at this point - we felt we were almost the only 'out of towners' in the valley. Which was quite amazing considering the scenery and adventure on offer. We had already had a bear sighting from a nice safe distance whilst doing a post-run river float with Fraser, as well as more bald eagle sightings than we could estimate a number for.

We had run through groves of old growth big cedar forests that would tell a story centuries long if they could talk. With a *Nuxalk* interpreter we had explored the petroglyphs of a sacred area of the forest that told a story millenia in the making - the local version of the creation stories of Canada's first peoples. After runs we had already feasted on locally caught grilled salmon and enjoyed evening beers at our lodge back in the valley with a hot tub and fire pit to ensure maximum post-run glow feeling. We had packed in a lot of trail time but now our time at the camp was a bit of a washout, and the weather obscured the nearby Hunlen Falls from view - falling over 850ft from the end of Turner Lake, they are amongst Canada's largest. But despite the rain we did some canoeing and running nonetheless and were secure in the knowledge we still had a couple more days exploring up our sleeve.

The group making the best of a wet, cold camping situation

After we ran out of the wild and back to the group vehicles we drove up and out of the Bella Coola valley, leaving its damp, maritime, temperate rainforest climate behind, and moving up on to the Chilcotin Plateau where summers are hotter and winters are colder, where the caribou march and the mosquitoes resemble sparrows. The locals' go-to mosquito joke is that there is not a single mosquito in the Chilcotin - they are all married with children. From a running perspective, the advantage of large and ferocious mosquitoes (I'm searching here, can there actually be an advantage of these dreadful creatures?) is that they are very effective at keeping you on the move and prevent any lapses into hiking or stopping for snacks - you are simply compelled to keep running. The mosquito's determination to bite becomes your determination to run. We experienced this on a stunning run into the vast Rainbow Range. A region where exploratory trips are better measured in weeks than days - just to run through a section of it and appreciate the scale was a joy. Thousands of feet above the Bella Coola valley the landscape was more sparsely forested, pocked with lakes, ponds and boggy areas. The weather was now finally cooperating - it seemed, yet again, that we had earned some sun and blue sky by previous suffering. Not only did we get the sun on our backs for our run in the Rainbow Range, later that day we appreciated the full scale of the place by air. An evening float plane ride - holding just 5 people plus the pilot at a time - took off from the lakeside lodge we were now staying at. It cruised over mountains and lakes, gliding over the glacial expanses of the Monarch Icefield, and later banked low over the now revealed Hunlen Falls so we could finally admire it. It was mesmerising. Its impressive size was amplified by how remote it was and by how few people got to see it. After the sightseeing plane ride we whiled away the evening on the deck by the lake, soaking in the sun, enjoying cold beers and warm hospitality from our hosts. We conducted our traditional award ceremony with home fashioned bear bell medals awarded to all the runners. So accustomed were we to the jingle of the bells everywhere we ran, we figured the runners might as well jingle all the way home with them. It was an ideal end to the trip.

Enjoying the sunshine - and watching a bear! - from the banks of the Bella Coola River

As the runners flew out back to Vancouver the next day Allison and I stood at the tiny airport and watched them depart. We still had to drive a couple of hours back down into Bella Coola Valley to return vehicles and tie up a few loose ends to the trip. But our work was done. We high fived and grinned at a job well done - relief and satisfaction flooded in. There had been many worries coming into the trip. Every first trip has unknowns but this trip in particular was more on us, more DIY, pulling together logistics that seemed to include a lot of plane rides always under weather threat, a lot of rough and ready trails always under bear threat. But that was in keeping with the frontier style of the place. One had to be hands-on in Bella Coola - there wasn't any other option. That was part of the intrinsic appeal and charm of the place. It wasn't the most polished destination and our runners most likely wouldn't end up there without us.

Our high five was just a couple of hours too early though. Fraser and his team were waiting back at his cabin with a barbecue and beers. Just a few minutes from the airport though, I managed to puncture a tyre on his passenger van - something we had been worried about all week on the rough gravel roads. Of course it would happen now. Allison was driving in convoy with the 4x4 truck and she circled back to find me underneath the van fighting with the mechanism to lower the spare wheel. Long story short, after a half an hour of sweating and struggling, a few dozen mosquito bites, a liberal application of swear words, and some very stubborn wheel nuts, I concluded I could not change the wheel. The moment of my deflation was absolute. We had no cell service and it was two hours back to Fraser, but with no other help nearby we abandoned the van and drove back in the 4x4. It should have been a triumphant arrival back to the cabin to mark the end of the first trip. Fraser was as excited as us at having delivered a running trip in his backyard - he had long wanted to diversify the typical visitor to the valley beyond bear viewing. He was the picture of barbecue contentment when we pulled up - shirt off, shades on, cold beer in a koozie in his hand, grill hot and ready for burgers beside him, he grinned widely as we walked across the lawn to join him. Then he saw our expressions, and glanced over our shoulders to the lack of van we had come back with. The barbecue was over and a van rescue mission was now deployed. One of those moments that is much funnier a year or so after the event. "End of trip high fives have been outlawed ever since." Allison concludes.

Wheel changing abilities aside, the feeling we had coming away from BC was one of knowing our place and our role. We were finally feeling confident in what it was that we should be offering as running guides. We were realising that we could offer hard to reach destinations, complicated logistics, more ambitious itineraries. We could consistently find the right people to make trips happen. We could find good local businesses to work with in the places that we went - the right kinds of accommodation, people with the right ethics and motivations. There was a skillset to what we were doing which, until that point, we had perhaps been a little bit self-conscious about recognising and appreciating.

Perhaps it seems surprising that this realisation was coming so late. But in some ways the business was just hitting its stride by the end of 2018 and through 2019. I had been added as the third full-time employee in July of 2018. I broke the news to Allison during the third installation of our Endurance Adventure Morocco trip just as we were crossing some snow fields below the Toubkal mountain refuge. "I think I'm out," I told her, referring to my full-time job at Spartan. "Yeah yeah, just let us know when you're serious," she replied dismissively, thinking that the mountain air was getting to me and I was just enjoying being away from my email inbox for a week. But as soon as we got off the mountain and back to connectivity I committed to the change and thankfully Allison and Gabe were ready to welcome me aboard.

Katie was also guiding more and more trips and starting to 'take point' on the Slovenia and Croatia trips besides the Bend and Tahoe trips. A fifth guide came into the fold when Kate Brun - Atlanta based, a bundle of positive energy and good vibes - made the transition from trip participant, to recruiter (as she pulled in more and more runners in the Atlanta area on subsequent trips), and finally became a team and family member. The team grew as the business grew and the addition of the British Columbia trip in 2019 took the total to 21 trips for the year and all of the destinations seemed to be in good demand from runners. We were busy and had lots of new plans and ideas in the works all the time. The network was always expanding. Interesting people and places were always just the next conversation away. The more one travels the more one realises how many places there are to travel. It is effectively an infinite list considering the limitation of one lifetime.

In searching out the off-the-beaten track places like Bella Coola there is always a slight apprehension. We felt this apprehension with Instagram posts and Strava updates - we were almost loath to share the secret places. Sometimes we preferred to keep certain details of trips under wraps - at least in the digital domain. We wanted them to stay undiscovered and private. We wanted to visit these places in a way that didn't damage them but celebrated them and cherished them. It felt like perhaps we were finding our niche within tourism and starting to figure out a positive way to interact with an industry so often maligned. With this feeling of finding our place and with the business on firm grounding at this stage our conversations often turned to 'what next.' There was never anything as official as a strategy meeting or a board meeting but these conversations crept up and got bounced around from time to time.

The zeitgeist surrounding the start-up business world would indicate that we should be at the rapid expansion stage of the business. The concept and product had been proofed and the key groundwork put in place. Now a typical start-up should seek outside investment and start using phrases like 'multiplier' and '10x growth' in their business plan. All that sounded a bit dreadful though. Instead Gabe describes the process as, "growing with our foot on the brake." Actively resisting growth at times. Holding it back so it was sustainable and controlled. We spent far more time talking about the type of lifestyle we wanted to have than how much money the company might be able to make. Wasn't that the whole point of building your own business - to create your own lifestyle? Wasn't that what inspired Allison and Gabe to take the leap of faith in the first place? People frequently asked about our plans to 'scale up' but we never had good answers to those questions and it seemed to us we were doing just fine at what was a boutique, niche level of tourism. We had full control and were active workers rather than managers. Did we want to become managers? Be at home in front of a laptop whilst new guides ran the trails and met the clients? It was a tricky question. Partly it relied on our continued appetite and enthusiasm for travel which is hard to assess into the future. Your motivations of today are unlikely to be your motivations of tomorrow. Did we want to add new types of tours alongside the existing ones - hiking or biking or corporate retreats of some other 'product diversification?' Again there was probably never a satisfactory or firm answer to this question.

We were also starting to chew on ideas about what our long-term goals were, what we wanted to achieve with the engaged and committed community we had built and the supportive and able network we had that now stretched across many countries. What impact could we have in the places we cared about? In the next few years but also in ten years or in twenty. Tourism has often dove-tailed into conservation or philanthropy - might we do something in that space? We were a bit nervous about this process as we didn't want to delve into something without doing it right. Little did we know that all these ideas and ruminations were about to hit a very hard unseen rock in the trail and progress was going to be halted. Making any impact starts with being able to survive.

| 11 |

2k to Go

I first started writing this chapter and this book in June 2020 - around 3 months into the Covid-19 crisis as it affected Rogue Expeditions and more than 6 months after the virus began to appear on the first news headlines coming out of China. It seems certain now that the virus will become one of those 'where were you when...' moments for all of us. Perhaps it will be even more profound and our lives will forever be divided into BC and AC - Before Covid and After Covid. But unlike single moments such as 9/11, Lady Diana's death or the result of the Brexit referendum, the initial phase of Covid-19 was a gathering news event over a longer period of time. So we can't all agree to pinpoint a particular moment but rather for each person there exists a personal 'holy shit' moment of realisation. Maybe it was a particular news headline, or someone you knew getting the virus, travel plans getting cancelled or your local schools getting closed. At some point you thought, huh, this is for real. This is happening.

For Rogue Expeditions, our 'holy shit' moment occurred on March 12th, 2020 somewhere right around 8.34 am Central European time. The evening previously, Gabe had caught a late news headline about all flights between Europe and the US being grounded effective midnight March 13th - the next day! He shared the headline in our group WhatsApp thread and then hit the hay for the night in Texas. Around 8.34am Allison was disembarking a flight from Houston to Frankfurt, discombobulated in the way that only 12 hours in a metal tube in the sky can cause discombobulation, and starting to plot her way to the next gate for a connecting flight to Marrakech. Around the same time I was emerging from a glorious 10 hour sleep cocooned under multiple blankets in a small *riad* in Imlil, 6000 feet up in the Atlas Mountains of Morocco. The window of my room was left open to let in the chilly morning mountain air and the sounds of the call to prayer like an alarm clock. The *imam* called for the second prayer of the day - the first is before sunrise and I for one sleep soundly through that - rousing me. I opened my phone. Our group WhatsApp thread reads:

03.30 Gabe: **"Ummm this could be a big problem"** sharing link to a headline of *'Trump suspends travel from Europe for 30 days as part of response to 'foreign' coronavirus'*

08.34 Allison: **"Well fuck. I guess that's it then."**

08.34 Allison: **"We need to cancel both"** - referring to our impending tour groups ready to arrive in Morocco in 48 hours' time.

08.44 Allison: **"@Sean give me a call when you get a chance"**

08.59 Sean: **"Fuck"** - feeling succinct with my first word of the day.

09.03 Sean: **"Allison where are you right now?"**

09.03 Sean: **"I'm free to chat"** - I was now 4 minutes more awake than 'fuck'.

09.04 Allison: **"Just landed Frankfurt"**

The biggest penny ever dropped during those 30 minutes from 08.34am to 09.04am on March 12th. It was thirty minutes of frantically scanning news headlines and government websites and trying to pinch ourselves - is this really happening? Rogue Expeditions had never in eighty something trips over seven years cancelled a trip for any reason. We had dodged and planned our way around terrorist attacks in Kenya, water crises in Cape Town, anti-government protests in Chile, wildfires in California and hiker murders in Morocco, but we were about to come unstuck by a foe unseen. We were about to start cancelling, and little did we know that cancelling would be in vogue for quite a while. Quite a while has turned into more than 12 months without running a trip. I simply wouldn't have believed that to be possible when the first lockdowns started. In fact, as I first started writing this book I frequently grew worried about my slow progress and that the pandemic would be over before I could finish! That I would miss the moment of the book, so to speak.

The breaking news that morning in March, whilst shocking, wasn't totally out of the blue of course. As with much of the rest of the world we had tracked the outbreak as it spread from China to Iran and then to Italy. We had run trips to Patagonia during January and February and noted the absence of Chinese travellers who were already restricted in their movements. There was a growing worm of worry growing in our minds but on some level we, along with many others, felt that things would get under control at some point - the right people would be working on it and know what to do. There had been outbreaks of SARS, MERS, Zika and Ebola before and the world had not stopped spinning. We assumed it would be an inconvenience at worst, but manageable. Again and again we were all about to have our assumptions and expectations turned on their head as things ran wildly out of control.

With hindsight, we cancelled those trips to Morocco just in the nick of time as we were mere hours away from the first runners heading to various airports to start their journeys to Marrakech. Many tourists became stuck in Morocco after all air traffic out of the country was grounded just a couple of days later. I scrambled to get on one of the last flights back out to Europe. Allison had already turned around in Frankfurt getting right back on board a flight back to Houston. Katie was already at home in Sydney, Australia with her fiancé wondering whether she'd be able to get back to the US in time for our scheduled summer trips. Our initial reaction as a guiding team was one of relief - it could have been much worse for us. We cancelled just in time and we were all home and safe and unaffected and would ride out the storm. As another trip got cancelled, and another, and the weeks turned to the months the emotions are best summarised though as a sense of loss. Lost experiences, lost memories that would never get created. Plans for newly developed trips to Nicaragua and Sweden got shelved and we cancelled the rest of our 2020 calendar month by month.

Our experience as guides by the beginning of 2020 was of returning to places we knew very well to work with people we trusted and loved. Hamid and his crew were like part of the family. Putting on our 'Morocco hats' for 2 or 3 months every year was part of the annual routine. I would pack my *djellaba*, get my Tinariwen playlist ready on Spotify, look forward to the big smile and big hug from Hamid outside Marrakech airport, look forward to my first egg and meatball *kefta* tagine, anticipate the places we had stayed before and my favourite runs, notice changes to the landscape from the previous season. Getting abruptly unplugged from this was unsettling. A further loss was the people that we wouldn't get to meet. Runners who had registered for trips and now might never get the chance to reschedule. There were lost opportunities for us and them to have potentially impactful experiences together. It may seem insignificant to highlight losses as ethereal as these in the face of real loss elsewhere - counted in loss of livelihoods and loss of life. But the truth for everyone is that they most keenly feel the losses that are closest and most immediate to them. The wiring of our evolutionary biology means that we generally don't deeply feel losses of the other people far away around the world. Or even in the next state or country over. This was a constant struggle of the pandemic. We were all alone with our own sense of loss and struggle. Try as we may to frame how fortunate we are - you probably are too if you're reading this book - and how much worse it could be, those feelings of *your own loss* never really get shaken off.

Thoughts of business survival were not really foremost in our mind during those initial months of the pandemic. We figured things might get going again by the summer or by the Fall. Gabe modeled a few different financial scenarios and came up with unpalatable but workable numbers. He and Allison were juggling the additional layer of complexity of leaving Austin and moving to Bend mid-lockdown - this time a permanent house to house move rather than an RV move. They were almost glad to have some free time to dedicate to that. We figured we would cut back every expense we could. Take as much of a pay cut as possible. Hope the runners registered for trips that were getting cancelled would take deferments instead of refunds - many did, and for that we are most thankful. Then we started to hope. We had to hope. Hope that a vaccine would come along. Hope there would be an end to all this with tourism resuming afterwards. If some visitor from the future came and told us in March 2020 that by March 2021 we wouldn't have run a single mile on a trip - well, maybe that would have punctured the hope and we would have gotten our CVs out and rode our separate directions into the sunset. It's the hope that kills you, they say. But it is also the hope that sustains you. Better to hope and be wrong than be pessimistic and be right.

Whilst we waited and hoped I started thinking about what a suspended pause for tourism really meant. The initial impact of the first lockdowns was startling - tourism as a whole ground to an unprecedented halt the world over. From the initial panic and fear there quickly emerged positive and hopeful narratives. News headlines initially celebrated the clearing smog in Delhi that meant the Himalaya were visible on the horizon for the first time in decades. As the gondolas and boats parked up in Venice, the waters cleared and fish and dolphins swam through sparkling clear canals. Animals revelled in the freedom of national parks freed from car traffic the world over, quickly wandering into areas they were usually never sighted. But quieter headlines followed. Gorillas were again getting poached in their mountain forests of Congo as ranger patrols were cut back due to plummeting tourism revenue with similar concerns in safari reserves across Africa. Millions of workers in developing countries around the world rely on the next planeload of tourists to arrive to sustain the taxis and the tuk-tuks, the hiking guides and the safari drivers, the cafes and the restaurants, the hostels and hotels. These workers often work day to day and hand to mouth and don't have a fallback option. Tourism has become integral and important to our global economy and society. The tourism economy is a redistribution between countries of higher wealth and countries of less wealth on a scale larger than charities and non-government organisations and aid distribution agencies - though in a double whammy, those are also losing revenue as rich countries reduce contributions in order to cope with mounting costs of the pandemic. We had never before contemplated what impact switching off the global tourism economy might have.

If you've read this far there is more than a passing chance that you like tourism and have future plans to see more of the world. So, indulge me to play for a moment in the sandbox of future tourism ideas. There have been many, many opinion pieces and commentaries on tourism during the last months (if you've missed them some Googling will catch you up) with change and reform being central themes and a 'new normal' for tourism being the agreed upon future. There is even a growing voice that would suggest that no international travel or tourism is acceptable anymore. That the pandemic has shown the folly of a hyper connected world and too much travel. Even if it didn't directly contribute to the initial virus outbreak the sheer scale of global travel and tourism probably aided and abetted the spread. This line of thought typically outlines that travel is too cheap and too available, generates too much carbon and is fundamentally unnecessary and superfluous. That the moral high ground is not to burn any carbon to go anywhere. Such absolutism is rarely workable though. The image of the tourist in the mind of a person espousing this absolutism may be something like this - hedonistic travellers seeking out the next selfie opportunity and more social media followers, shallowly interacting with places for the pure purpose of immediate gratification. They want to travel cheaper, faster, more and are irrevocably linked to cheaper and cheaper flights from Ryanair to Southwest, spring break weeks and full moon parties, bigger cruise ships, multinational hotel chains and industrial scale tourism schemes in places like Mexico's Riviera Maya or Spain's Canary Islands. There is some truth to this stereotype, but it only shows one side of the story and we can easily counter it by describing a different type of traveller. Someone who loves to travel and has done so fairly frequently but cherishes it each time as the first time. A traveller who offsets the carbon from their journey. Lives frugally and lightly upon the earth when not travelling. Who recognizes the food for the soul that travel provides and comes away from each experience fulfilled and changed, challenged and enlightened. Travel to this person has been paramount in their personal development and their understanding of the world around them. With their tourist dollars they patronise locally owned businesses, contribute to worthy causes they are exposed to during their travels, and ensure that their 'dollars and cents' impact on the place they visit is fair and just. This is probably not the picture of tourism that most anti-tourism people conjure up. So, is the answer to travel freely and plentifully or not at all? The answer, of course, as in all things in life is somewhere in the middle. The correct answer is rarely black and white. More often there is a need to find compromise and nuance. There exists a spectrum of travellers and of types of tourism. All parts of the spectrum will feel a pressure to change and adapt post-pandemic and all parts have a role to play going forward.

As more and more opinion pieces came out and the months of the anthropause grew longer I searched for answers to the current moment. Tourism has undoubtedly been on an unprecedented rise in recent years, but it has long roots stretching back centuries. To the Florence Dixie Victorian era who valued exploration and adventure - as well as countryside convalescence popularised in places like Ireland and Scotland by the British aristocratic class. But even beyond to religious pilgrimages to Rome or the Holy Lands which have been ongoing for many centuries. It is the scale nowadays which is different though. And the democratisation of knowledge. With Google Flights and Kayak, TripAdvisor and Lonely Planet, Booking.com and Airbnb, anyone anywhere can travel. Yet amongst this proliferation of information another movement is forming. The ideas have been bouncing around for a few years, first termed eco-tourism and then becoming sustainable tourism and in their latest iteration becoming regenerative tourism. The ideas have manifested in different ways from hotels that are off-grid or carbon neutral, to restaurants that are farm to table and locally sourced food, or carbon offsetting schemes that plant trees that will capture more carbon than was released by a flight or boat journey. Alone none of the solutions are complete. There are flaws to be found in any of them. They are all getting at the notion that travel and tourism can be done better or at a minimum less harmfully. Together, these ideas and this thinking gets towards the idea of a mindset shift.

To help sharpen up my thinking amongst all the opinion pieces in the media I had read, I spoke (on Zoom of course) to a key figure in the growing regenerative tourism movement who left a couple of key thoughts ringing in my ears. The first thought was that starting to think about these things is already part of the solution. This is important. Awareness and thinking are the beginning. Not the whole solution of course, but a start, and that's ok. We simply don't have all the answers yet. Carbon offsetting for example is not perfect. People are quick to point out that millionaires can't just pay for endless trees to get planted - perhaps they should fly their private jets less. This is a fair point. But doesn't mean carbon offsetting has no value at all as a solution, and doesn't mean it can't improve and evolve over time until true carbon neutral travel can be devised.

The second thought from my conversation was that we cannot know the cash value or carbon value of the cultural and ideological exchange of tourism. This opens a larger thought. We can't reduce tourism to a number of dollars. It isn't just an economic exchange. When it is done well, there is something more happening. In the exchange between the tourist and the resident it is a two-way street. Ideas are going both ways - more than either party possibly realises. Elements of culture and ways of looking at the world are being transferred. The 'other' suddenly becomes a fellow human. For example, anyone who travels regularly becomes acutely aware of their own nationality - the little book they have to hold in their hand at the airport. They hear the language they speak with when talking to someone who doesn't seem to understand. The out of body moment of seeing oneself in a foreign place - how do I appear to everyone else here? What do they see? This moment of reflection can be incredibly useful. This moment enables people to access the power of empathy when traveling. An immediate ability to relate to a new place and culture through the commonality of basic human experience. Struggles, aspirations, failures, successes, hopes, dreams. Every human everywhere, regardless of circumstance, goes through these things. At times some new cultural quirk will be a step too far for your empathy and you'll feel totally out of sync and out of place. Those are the glorious moments of immersion, treading waters of truly new phenomena. It is probably more likely that you've contemplated the negative side of the social and ideological exchange of tourism. Corrupting and bad cultural memes coming from western societies - from fast food to Facebook. But the truth is that the cultural exchange between the people of the world has been going on always and forever. Since the first upright hominids walked out of Africa and started comparing stone tools and fur clothes. There was no beginning to this process, no static cultural origin, and there won't be an end. We can only hope that better ideas, as judged by their net positive impact on visitors and residents, survive and spread over the fullness of time. That the ideological exchange remains broad and open, rich and diverse. That we each try to play a positive role in this process, no matter how small.

The final key thought from my conversation was that if people seem to have an innate desire to explore and travel then perhaps we can harness this urge. Work with underlying human nature than against. Guilting everyone to stay home forever seems a tough task. Why not harness the mobilised dollars towards good. Can regenerative tourism be an engine for positive change? Both in an economic sense and a net positive social impact for all parties. A lofty goal no doubt, but the answer can quite possibly be yes. But there is no silver bullet. Tourism has no central governance that can issue a command and no central set of principles that can be updated. So, the answers will take many shapes and forms. Travellers will in effect form the system of regulation as they choose to patronise certain elements of tourism and not others, just as they do with products in a supermarket or choosing running clothes from a more sustainable producer. Each traveller can in effect keep their own scorecard and try to do the best they can. In the same vein many tourism operators must attempt the same. Many already do. In terms of who they work with and patronise, in the message they put into the world, into the impact of the trips they run. Many companies in the adventure tourism sector in particular use their platforms to amplify good messages or contribute to a good cause - be it environmentally focused, or women's education in sub-Saharan Africa, or mosquito nets and anti-malaria medication - whatever issue it is that resonates for them. Customers are coming to know how to tell real caring companies with a genuine mission rather than those with a marketing or PR gimmick. We are all attaining more literacy in this regard all the time.

After my musings, it was time to turn this thinking back on myself. If nothing else, the pandemic gave everyone time to do a stock check and bearing check on their own lives - what is the path forward? Overall it seems obvious that tourism is going to bounce back. It may change and adapt but it won't go away. Approaching the future with these thoughts of regenerative tourism in mind are quite exciting. The opportunities are clear to see. The chance to have an impact or support a cause. The motivation to reach these opportunities is even greater than before - greater than simply the motivation of a livelihood or successful business. With Rogue we were already on a good path and open to continued evolution and change - it seems plausible that small-scale, well considered, flexible and responsive tourism could be a path forward.

Small group running trips serve as a vehicle for a more immersive sort of tourism. It tends to be an equalizing, barrier-breaking activity both amongst our group members themselves and amongst the communities we encounter. Every place on earth has runners, and nearly everyone on earth has some level of familiarity with it; consider the local reception to a foreigner driving through a Moroccan village with a camera pointed out the window compared to what happens when a group of foreigners goes running through. We get smiles, laughs, cheers, foot races with kids - instant interaction, very little suspicion. Our runners see, hear and interact with these places up close, in real life rather than just observing through a bus window. The running becomes a conversation starter with literally everyone the group encounters throughout the trip, everywhere we go. This tangible type of experience seems fertile ground into which to plant the seeds for positive ideas.

Dani and Kristen pick up enthusiastic new running partners in a village near the Tizi n Test mountain pass, Morocco.

For tourists and tourism operators there may be an increased requirement for more careful navigation of the tourism space. A need to continually update their moral arithmetic and a continued strive towards more sustainable and even regenerative tourism. That feels like an exciting sort of pressure though. An opportunity rather than a burden. But ultimately the rubber will only meet the road on all these thoughts and ideas if we can ever get back on the road again. Whilst thoughts of business survival might not have been utmost a year ago during the start of the pandemic, they are now. But there is cause for optimism. Light is appearing at the end of the tunnel.

I for one am ready to travel again. It isn't something you can stop easily. It is often said that travel is an education. If we drill down on that thought, we expose that it is actually true and not just a post-card quote. By analogy consider the learning of a language, or a musical instrument. The joy comes when the learning process starts to click into place. Different elements come together after the first attempts and all of sudden those verb conjugations are finally happening and you're saying full sentences in Spanish or Mandarin, you're using both hands on the piano or finally nailing that barre chord on the guitar. Those are the great moments in learning. When things click and the learning jumps forward. With travel it really is similar. Journey by journey, locally and internationally, you patch together a network of places you know and add layers of knowledge. You become a sort of an amateur travel scholar touching on anthropology, geography, world history, religion, languages, music and dance, cuisine and celebratory feasts, and much more besides. You uncover more of the areas of the map that are uncharted to you and become more and more of a world scholar - seeing connections in everything and feeling a citizen of the world, a part of it all. The more you learn the more you want to learn, and the more you realise how much you don't know. You'll never finish the study and that's ok. Along the way the running just fires up the neurons and justifies that big dinner at the end of the day.

* * *

In mid-December 2019, before the pandemic bit, we held a Rogue Expeditions end of year party in Austin. We held it at Rogue Running HQ in Austin which was now more of a warehouse than a cramped training room. Many of the same elements remained - whiteboards covered in training plans, funky runner smell from the lost and found section, thrum of energy every day with hundreds of dedicated runners passing through the doors - but the scale was bigger now. The community had grown so the space had to as well. The warehouse afforded a large airy space complete with retail area for running apparel and big open area for training drills and strength work. We filled this space with the familiar faces of friends who had been on trips with us. Dozens and dozens of runners arrived, lured by the beer and tacos on offer no doubt, but lured principally by the chance to connect with other people like them. Many knew each other from the local running scene, whilst others travelled in from around Texas and the US and even one attendee Christina who flew in from the UK! Some had met in Morocco or some other far-off trip, many compared which trips they had been on and exchanged stories and anecdotes and plotted which trip they would like to go on next. Allison, Gabe and I said a few words of thanks, shared a few funny stories from the road that year, and indulged a few upcoming plans for a big 2020 - our biggest year yet. With the addition of BC, we climbed to 21 trips in 2019 and had 23 planned for 2020 including new itineraries in Ireland and Morocco and some teasing details on our potential new destinations. We shared video messages from those around the world who helped make the Rogue trips happen but couldn't be there in person - Katie said hello from Australia, Kate flew down to Austin to say hello in person, Hamid shared some words from Morocco, Tone from Slovenia, Ciaran chimed in from Ireland, Sergio from Patagonia. Kinuthia was in Austin and said hello in person. It was an amazing evening. Everyone together. Conversations flying. Exactly the type of occasion the pandemic has taken away. A room full of friends and stories and energy. At that moment the future was full of promise. This is the moment that we as a business shall pause on before we resume. The energy and excitement, the community and togetherness, the stories shared and the adventures yet to come. The feeling in that room that night hasn't gone anywhere, it has just been put on ice for a little while.

* * *

'2k to go'

On our trips in Morocco we often have 3 or 4 or 5 Land Cruisers to accommodate transportation of our larger groups. They come in very handy during runs as the drivers space out along the route and offer water, dates, nuts and other snacks to passing runners. As the mileage climbs runners will invariably wonder 'where is that blasted finish line?' In the absence of Gabe or Allison or Katie or I they'll often ask our drivers.

"How many more miles?" They pant at the driver whilst snatching a handful of dried apricots and filling their water bottle. The stock response from all our drivers, on all our runs, at any arbitrary point of the run will be:

"2k to go!"

The beauty of this moment is that the drivers don't know how far a mile is, and the runners often don't know how far a kilometre is. The drivers often don't know or care where the finish line of the run is either. To them these runners have travelled a long way to run, so who cares how much farther to run there is? More is better, right? The drivers have come to know that '2k to go' gets a favourable response from the runners. They almost always smile, say thanks, and run onwards down the road to the distant finish line.

* * *

So how long until this pandemic is over and we can travel again, I hear you ask? Well, let's just say that there is 2k to go, then keep putting one foot in front of the other.

ACKNOWLEDGEMENTS

Writing this book has been a cathartic break from pandemic worries and a highly enjoyable process for myself, Allison and Gabe. A happy moment to indulge in looking back during a time when looking forward has been fraught with uncertainties, and to reflect upon all of the people and places that have been a part of our story for the past nine years.

From the intrepid Austin runners who put their faith in those first tentative trips in 2013 and 2014 and the supportive friends and family who cheered us on, to the local partners who continually help transform our big ideas into reality and everyone who has stuck with and supported us throughout the unthinkable challenges of the pandemic, thank you. To Ruth England, who trusted Allison & Gabe to attach the Rogue name onto our half-baked idea and then run with it - none of this would have happened without the support of you and the Rogue Running community! To our brother Hamid - meeting you was one of the most pivotal moments in our lives, and we can't wait to share many, many more adventures together, *inshallah*. We are profoundly, eternally grateful to everyone who has been a part of this journey so far.

An additional thank you to everyone who consented to be mentioned in the book and to the many who provided memories and quotes - we could fill another book with anecdotes and stories but have to save some material for in-person renditions! We can't wait to get back on the road and make all new memories with you all again soon.

Special thanks to Frances Day whose editorial guidance and copy editing carefully nudged a tatty document towards an actual story. She very probably prevented this from being another unfinished start lurking forgotten in Google Drive, and she taught me how to write the word 'I' which was a tricky business to begin with.

The author in his happy place, the High Atlas gîte

ABOUT THE AUTHOR

Sean Meehan is a guide with Rogue Expeditions, an Austin-based run-centric adventure travel company. Over the past decade he has created and produced running events and adventures in over 25 countries.

Originally from County Fermanagh, Northern Ireland, he writes from his current home in Bavaria or wherever his travel duffel happens to be. Venture is his first book.

CPSIA information can be obtained
at www.ICGtesting.com
Printed in the USA
FSHW020447220521
81693FS